Advance Praise for
From Container to Kitchen

I have been reading the gardening books of master grower D. J. Herda for more than twenty years. His latest — *From Container to Kitchen* — is very likely his best. It goes to show that anyone who wants a garden can have a garden, no matter where he or she lives! It's an invaluable guide filled with fun facts and useful tips. Pick up a copy as soon as you can. You won't regret it.

— Don Bacue, former executive editor,
International Features Syndicate

With *From Container to Kitchen*, D. J. Herda shows us not only the importance of eating healthy and saving money, but the joy and peace to be found in creating sustainability. This book is among the best I've read on the actual importance of "getting back to nature," no matter where you live.

— Michielle DJ Beck, Author, Content Creator,
Editor (www.michiellebeck.com)

From Container to Kitchen is a refreshing twist on the how-to approach, combining practical information along with DJ's personal experience with and love for container gardening. If you're not a container gardener now, you will be after you read this book!

— Annette Ranald, author and attorney.

GROWING
FRUITS AND
VEGETABLES
IN POTS

from
container
to kitchen

D.J. HERDA

NEW SOCIETY PUBLISHERS

Cataloging in Publication Data:
A catalog record for this publication is available
from the National Library of Canada.

Printed in Canada by Friesens.
First printing March 2010.

Paperback ISBN: 978-0-86571-665-0
Inquiries regarding requests to reprint all or part of *From Container to Kitchen*
should be addressed to New Society Publishers at the address below.

To order directly from the publishers, please call toll-free (North America)
1-800-567-6772, or order online at www.newsociety.com

Any other inquiries can be directed by mail to:
New Society Publishers
P.O. Box 189, Gabriola Island, BC V0R 1X0, Canada
(250) 247-9737

New Society Publishers' mission is to publish books that contribute in fundamental ways to building an ecologically sustainable and just society, and to do so with the least possible impact on the environment, in a manner that models this vision. We are committed to doing this not just through education, but through action. This book is one step toward ending global deforestation and climate change. It is printed on Forest Stewardship Council-certified acid-free paper that is **100% post-consumer recycled** (100% old growth forest-free), processed chlorine free, and printed with vegetable-based, low-VOC inks, with covers produced using FSC-certified stock. New Society also works to reduce its carbon footprint, and purchases carbon offsets based on an annual audit to ensure a carbon neutral footprint. For further information, or to browse our full list of books and purchase securely, visit our website at: www.newsociety.com

NEW SOCIETY PUBLISHERS
www.newsociety.com

Mixed Sources
Cert no. SW-COC-001271
© 1996 FSC

FSC

Contents

Introduction

The first book I ever published on the subject of growing plants in containers was one of the first books I ever published *period*. It was called *Growing Trees Indoors*, and it was a runaway hit, coming within a few hundred thousand copies of making the *New York Times* Bestsellers' List.

The book earned me, back in 1979, nearly universal praise (someone from Wisconsin's *Mt. Horeb Mail* said it was a damned fine book, with pictures and everything) and garnered me a fortune in royalties, totaling nearly $800, if memory serves me correctly. It also taught me a valuable lesson about the concept of growing plants in containers: People weren't ready for it.

Today, more than 30 years later, all that has changed. For one thing, I'm just about exactly 30 years older. For another, I'm a whole lot smarter. And, finally, people *are* ready for it.

Why the change in attitude? Why is today the right time for a book on growing plants in containers — and not only plants, but *edible* plants, fruits of the womb, sustainable-growth harvestable manna — as opposed to a book on container gardening more than three decades ago?

Filling a Void

Well, for starters, more people than ever before are living in urban environments. Apartments, condominiums, spider holes stacked neatly one on top of another — just about any habitable space is being inhabited. That means that more people than ever before are no longer able to enjoy the benefits of traditional gardening. It's difficult to walk out the back door, grab a shovel and begin rooting around in the yard when the "yard" consists of three cubic feet of poured concrete separating the high rise apartment building next door from the one in which you live.

The fact that most people don't have access to large yards or corner lots or sprawling acres in the countryside anymore doesn't negate their innate desire to garden, of course. It only makes their desire to garden that much stronger. The gardening urge is genetically implanted in our souls. Gardening is as old an activity as modern mankind. Before ancient hunters came gardeners. Before ancient real-estate brokers came gardeners. Before even Rupert Murdoch came gardeners. In fact, the only human activity to precede gardening was gathering. Gatherers wandered from area to area, scrounging up enough fruits and berries, seeds and nuts to sustain them throughout their lifetime, which must have averaged fifteen or twenty years. And many of them were gatherers only because they hadn't yet discovered Burpee's online catalog!

Today, people feel a need to get back to their prehistoric origins, to return to their genetically programmed basics — something that is difficult to do when you live in New York or Chicago or Los Angeles, damned near impossible to do when you live in a three-story brownstone or a high-rise megalith spiraling hundreds of feet above Lake Michigan.

A Healthier Alternative

People also feel a need to garden because they're more health-conscious than their ancestors were. They're better informed about the world around us. With all of the periodic stories about tainted fruits and vegetables — including salmonella, which, contrary to popular belief, does not come exclusively from salmon — who wouldn't worry? With all the tales about produce laced with toxins and heavy metals, about irradiated and otherwise diminished foodstuffs of questionable nutritional value and similar concerns, it's suddenly not only socially expedient but also physiologically critical to find a source of clean, fresh, vitamin-rich produce. At least it is for anyone who doesn't consider Fruit Loops and Bloomin' Onions to be among the US Department of Health's top two food groups.

Yet today when you visit the produce section of your local supermarket, you find apples that were picked in Madagascar three weeks ago; tomatoes that were plucked green, gassed and trucked up from Mexico four weeks ago; bananas that were picked unripened from a plantation in Costa Rica five weeks ago; and bell peppers whose origins and date of harvest are still a mystery.

Stand back and watch as little kids fondle the produce — right after holding their pet frogs and iguanas. You see adults coughing and sneezing into their hands before hefting a dozen tomatoes and returning them to the stand as not quite suitable. You observe employees hoisting cardboard boxes from stacks of other cardboard boxes sitting on the floor and emptying their contents into bins marked "Special — $2.79 a Pound."

Fresh, healthful fruit and produce? You tell me.

Cutting Costs

People are also turning increasingly to gardening because they worry about the high cost of shopping. I remember a time not long ago when meat was the most expensive thing you could buy at your local

This dwarf nectarine tree adapts nicely to container growth and bears full-sized fruit every summer

supermarket and vegetarians were considered frugal, if not outright weird. Today, fresh fruits and vegetables rival, and in many cases surpass, the cost of meat — thanks in great part to spiraling harvest and delivery costs — and vegetarians present a glowing portrait of people who know something the rest of us don't. Of course, they're still considered weird, but that's another story.

With the rising cost of produce such as we are experiencing, how can we cope? Who wants to take out a second mortgage on the condo merely to buy fresh fruits and vegetables? Who wants to give up financial liquidity for a few more years of physical and emotional well-being? Or could there be another way?

The Time Is Now

Finally, I felt the time was right for a book on growing plants in containers because I need the money. Had that original tome about growing trees indoors that I wrote lo! those many years ago sold better, I probably wouldn't have had to write another book on container gardening *ever*.

But that was not the case. I abhor refined sugars and starches; I hate paying through the nose for things that I could be supplying for myself and my family for next to no cost; and I want to put all of the knowledge I have gained about container gardening to good use. What choice did I have but to tackle the ultimate book on fruit and vegetable gardening?

There are other reasons for the timeliness of this book, of course. For one, technology has advanced to the point where, today, no-yard gardening is easier than ever. Modern inventions (mere pipedreams back during the early days of garden writing) and new discoveries about effective horticultural techniques make growing fruit and vegetables in pots more practical than ever before. For another, new varieties of plants — both fruits and vegetables — called cultivars (short for "cultivated varieties") make container gardening much easier and more successful than in the good old days B.C. (Before Containers).

Thus was born the concept for this book.

But those are not the only reasons for growing fruit and vegetables in pots — not by a long shot. There are others, and I'll be presenting them to you within the next few pages of this guide. I'll tell you some of the things you can do and grow with a minimum of knowledge, a minimum of space and a maximum of enjoyment. I'm even going to tell you how container gardening can not only change your life, but also very possibly *save* it.

Here you're going to learn which fruits and vegetables grow best in pots, which varieties outperform their less robust cousins, how to plant and nurture your crops from planting to harvest, how to build your own best recipe for gardening success and how get the message out to others; the time is right for container gardening.

And you're going to read about it all right here.

Tomatoes (*solanum lycopersicum*)

Habit: Trellis, cherry and plum

Cultivars: The following tomato cultivars are recommended for container gardening. Most are indeterminate (trellis or vining) except for Celebrity and Small Fry.

- *Improved:* Better Boy, Better Bush Improved, Big Beef, Celebrity, Early Girl, Park's Whopper, Terrific
- *Cherry type:* Juliet, Small Fry, Super Sweet 100, Sweet Million
- *Plum type:* Viva Italia
- *Trellis type:* Tropic

Always choose varieties with disease resistance. Fusarium wilt is a common disease that can destroy a whole tomato crop. Many varieties are resistant to this disease. This is indicated by the letters VF after the cultivar name. VFN means the plants are resistant to Verticillium, Fusarium and nematodes; VFNT adds tobacco mosaic virus to the list.

Seed or Transplants: Both

Pot Size: Medium to large

Water: Water regularly, allowing soil to dry out between waterings.

Comments: Tomatoes come in a wide range of sizes, tastes, colors, harvest times, growing habits and purposes. They are also available in your choice of a wide range of heirloom (mostly true from seed) and varietal hybrid types in trellis (i.e., spreading or indeterminate), bush (upright or determinate) or patio (compact ultra-determinate). Add to all of that multiple colors and sizes, and it's no wonder that tomatoes are among the world's best-suited vegetables for container growing. They are also among the easiest to grow and are valuable garden plants in that they require

Tomatoes (*Solanum lycopersicum*)

relatively little space for large production. Each plant, properly cared for, yields 10 to 15 pounds or more of fruit.

Varieties: The varieties of tomato plants available may seem overwhelming, but they can be summed up by several major types:

Midget, patio or *dwarf* tomato varieties have very compact vines and grow well in hanging baskets or other containers. The tomatoes produced may be, but are not always, the cherry-type (1-inch diameter or less).

Cherry tomatoes have small fruits often used for snacking or in salads. Plants of cherry tomatoes range from dwarf (Tiny Tim) to seven-footers (Sweet 100).

Compact or *determinate* tomato plants grow to a certain size, set fruit and then gradually die. Most of the early-ripening tomato varieties are determinate and will not produce tomatoes throughout the entire summer. Because of their compact habit, they make excellent container candidates.

Beefsteak types are large-fruited. These are usually late to ripen.

Paste tomatoes have small pear-shaped fruits with very meaty interiors and few seeds. They are a favorite for canning.

Orange or yellow tomatoes may be available to you only by growing your own.

Winter storage tomatoes are set out later in the season than most tomatoes and the fruits are harvested partially ripe. If properly stored, they will stay fresh for 12 weeks or longer. Though the flavor does not equal that of summer vine-ripened tomatoes, many people prefer them to grocery store tomatoes in winter.

Seeds: Plant seeds to a depth approximately twice the thickness of the seed; water and tamp soil firmly. Cover pot with a clear plastic container or wrap, and wait for germination. Keep soil moist but not saturated, and keep pot out of direct sunlight to avoid overheating. Uncover at the first sign of sprouts. Thin to approximately one plant per six square inches when second set of leaflets forms on plants.

Transplants: Remove all lower leaf stems except top two levels. Place plantlet diagonally in a trough three inches deep in the soil, leaving only the upper two levels of leaves exposed, and tamp firmly. Roots will grow from the covered plant stem, as well as from the plant's root ball, creating a stronger, healthier, more drought-resistant plant.

Soil: The desired soil pH for tomatoes is between 5.8 and 6.5. Tomatoes are heavy feeders. Use a starter solution for transplants and feed throughout the season with a low-nitrogen fertilizer to encourage greater fruit production and less foliar growth.

Insects: Watch for spider mites and aphids in particular, as well as green horn worm, if plant is kept outdoors. **Solutions:** Spray plant with biologically friendly non-detergent soap mixed with water (1T per gallon water). Worms may be picked off and disposed of by hand. Wear gloves if you're squeamish.

Diseases: Fusarium wilt, which attacks and can kill young plants, is a notorious fungal problem, although in recent years, the susceptibility to the wilt has been greatly reduced in modern varieties. The disease is first marked by the yellowing of older leaves, then bright yellowing from top to bottom of the plant, often affecting only one branch. Sometimes the leaves droop and curve downward. Infected plants most often wilt and die. **Solutions:** Use *Trichoderma harzianum*, a harmless additive, as a soil drench to suppress root pathogens on newly sown seeds, transplants and established plants. Also, use only sterilized garden or potting soil of medium alkalinity (pH 6.5 to 7.0). It's a good idea to keep your plants well ventilated, either naturally or through use of a small electric fan to keep the air around the plants circulating.

Health Benefits: In the arena of food and phytonutrient studies, the star of the show over the past decade or more has been the lycopene in tomatoes. For years this carotenoid has been the subject of numerous studies for its antioxidant and cancer-preventing properties. The antioxidant function of lycopene helps protect human cells and other physiological structures in the body from oxygen damage and has been linked in human research to the protection of DNA (our basic genetic material) found inside white blood cells.

Another antioxidant role played by lycopene is in the prevention of heart disease. In contrast to many other food phytonutrients, the effects of which have been studied only in animals, *lycopene* from tomatoes has been studied in humans for years. The results show that it is a powerful combatant to a wide range of cancers, including colorectal, prostate, breast, endometrial, lung and pancreatic.

While lycopene may play an important role in the growth of healthy tomato plants, it isn't the only shining star that gives this food a growing reputation for being on the front line of defense against disease. Recent research suggests that scientists are finding that a wide range of nutrients in tomatoes — and not merely lycopene — are responsible for promoting human health, with additional studies being launched daily.

Ready for the Kitchen: When fruit is fully formed and deep in color. May also be harvested green before the first killing frost and allowed to ripen at room temperature (not refrigerated) for up to eight weeks, although I have in the past ripened some in this manner for up to four months. It takes 55 to 105 days to maturity depending on the tomato variety, so know what you're planting in advance. Pick fruit when it is fully vine-ripened but still firm. Picked tomatoes should be kept away from direct sun.

Annual Savings: Approximately $130 per year per person on average.

Gardening for your Health

For years, people have understood that life in the fast lane can take its toll. A once increasingly urbanized and mechanized society has become an increasingly "technocratic" world in which the cost of maintaining high-stress jobs (getting to the office at nine, listening to your supervisors talk about what a great job you're doing and how you're on the fast track up the corporate ladder, and coming home again at five) is proving to be enormous. Emotional stress runs rampant. Violent crime is on the rise. Mental health manifestations are increasingly more the exception than the rule.

Let's face reality. As a society, we're a mess. Working parents are short-tempered and irascible. Nonworking parents are short-tempered and irascible. Children are short-tempered and irascible. Cable television, videos and digital diversions merely exacerbate the problem, making us *all* short-tempered and irascible.

A growing number of medical researchers insist that stressful jobs can be combated successfully through physical activity. An active body, or so runs the thought process, places a stressed mind at rest. Thus was born the concept behind the modern health club. We *homo sapiens* are nothing if not an ingenious species, spending what few expendable hours we have each week with someone who gets paid to tell us which machines to use to accomplish which goals to gain which benefits, none of which ever seems to work quite according to plan.

But, hey, wait a minute, you say. Do we really *need* to go to the gym to get into shape? I mean, isn't gardening good physical exercise? Don't you work up a sweat transplanting a hybrid tomato seedling from its peat-pot container into a clay pot on your patio? Don't you work up a sweat moving a five-inch potted begonia into its new twelve-inch home?

Well, okay, maybe not. Maybe the healthful aspect of gardening isn't all about physical exercise. It could be, of course, depending upon the amount and the degree of gardening to which you expose your Type-A personality. But even when it's not overtly physical, gardening nonetheless exercises portions of the brain that otherwise may lie fallow (sorry, I couldn't resist).

And getting to work outdoors — even if it's to pick up a bag of soil from the back seat of the car and carry it up the steps to your apartment — works wonders for the psyche. Don't even stop to question what working on the patio or veranda in the sunshine and the wind does for your spirits and well being.

"In addition to the health benefits, getting your exercise outdoors improves mental focus, emotional power and your connection to the environment — something scientists call the *biophilia* effect, or the need to be in nature or the natural world," according to Tina Vindum, who has created a get-fit-outdoors initiative built around gardening.[1] Vindum is a professional trainer who leads the only accredited outdoor fitness program in the US.

She recently teamed with power equipment manufacturer Husqvarna to launch "Outdoor Power!" an initiative designed to encourage people to use their outdoor projects to feel good and get fit. She believes strongly that gardening helps people not only get and stay physically fit, but also grow emotionally from their experiences.

Widening View

She is not alone in her beliefs. Hundreds of thousands of others are discovering the healthful and life-lengthening benefits of gardening, as well.

The first thing that Gene Gach does each morning after climbing out of bed is to walk out into his garden, where he surveys the four dozen pots of bromeliads he has growing next to the house. After that he takes a deep breath and admires the modest backyard of his Los Angeles-area home. He takes in the rose bushes and a stand of Chinese bamboo he began from a single small stalk years ago.

On many mornings he watches the birds swoop around, chirping noisily for food. A small rabbit he's teaching to eat lettuce out of his hand occasionally pays a visit. Several squirrels skitter around, begging for handouts.

Gach is never stingy. After tending to his flocks, he often plays a round of golf with his wife, followed by lunch and a couple hours of gardening. It's the gardening that is the joy of his life.

"Days like this leave me with an incredible sense of peace and serenity," he said when asked what he enjoys most about nature. "When I stand in my garden I can feel the seeds under the earth, everything growing, and I have a connection to all of life."[2]

Gach, who retired several years ago from a career as a press agent and corporate fundraiser, may sound like a fanatic, like an ex-hippie right out of the history of Haight-Ashbury, someone who never quite outgrew the "groovy" sights and sounds of the peace movement and getting back to nature and the Great Outdoors.

He's not. He is 87 years old and the author of a recently released autobiography espousing his approach to life and what he says makes the most sense to him.

"The doctor who gave me a recent cardiac stress test couldn't believe it," he said. "'You're twice my age,' he told me, 'and your blood pressure is lower on the treadmill than mine is sitting down.'"[3]

What makes Gach so spry? It's impossible to say for sure, but he believes — and numerous physicians and others might agree — that his connection to nature plays the greatest role.

Edward O. Wilson, a naturalist and Pulitzer Prize winner, is one of those others who concurs. Wilson, who coined the term *biophilia* (a love of living things), says that people have an affinity for nature because we ourselves are natural beings. As part of nature, we prefer looking at the beauty of nature — at flowers and grass and trees and shrubs — rather than at concrete and steel. As part of nature, we are connected to the Great Outdoors. Even more so, he believes, we are nurtured and restored by it.

The restorative benefits of nature, an increasingly large number of experts believe, can make a marked difference in people's lives. Nature can lower blood pressure, boost immune-system function and reduce stress — all positive benefits that relate to a longer, healthier, happier life.

To reap these and other benefits, you needn't be a multi-millionaire living in a large mansion with a staff of professional gardeners at your beck and call. In fact, just the opposite. Simply give in to your love of plants, pop a few seeds into some soil or look out the window (or even at a photograph, as remarkable as it sounds) to reconnect with your own roots.

The Power of Nature

A landmark study by Roger S. Ulrich, published in the April 27, 1984, issue of *Science* magazine, found strong evidence that nature helps people to heal. Ulrich, a pioneer in the field of therapeutic environments at Texas A&M University, learned that recovering gallbladder patients who looked out the window at a view of trees had significantly shorter hospital stays, fewer complaints and a need for fewer pain pills than those who looked out of their windows at a brick wall.[4]

More recently, studies presented at the 1999 Culture, Health and Arts World Symposium in England found similar benefits to looking out upon nature. One study, conducted in Uppsala, Sweden, followed 160 postoperative heart patients who were divided into three groups. The patients in the groups were asked to look at a photograph of a landscape, at an abstract work of art or at no picture at all.

Those who looked at the landscape had a lower incidence of anxiety and a greater tolerance of everyday aches and pains. They also spent on average one day less in the hospital per illness than a control group of patients in the same study.

Those patients who viewed the abstract art, however, actually felt sicker: the overall health of those viewing the abstraction was worse than those who saw no art at all. They were more anxious and initially took more pain killers than did the control patients,[5] which may be a valuable lesson for our Department of Defense: "Promise them anything, but give them a Picasso!"

Similar studies have found that looking at various nature scenes produces a marked decline in systolic blood pressure in five minutes or less, even when the patient is looking only at a *poster* of nature, according to Ulrich. Viewing nature, he observed, can also aid recovery from stress as measured by changes in the brain's electrical activity, muscle tension, respiration and shifts in emotional states, all of which may be linked to improved immune-system function. A stronger immune system, in turn, can help to protect people from a wide range of diseases and shorten their recovery times when stricken by a serious physical or emotional malady.

Ulrich goes so far as to speculate that the results of his studies are more than suggestive reactions to pleasurable stimuli. He believes that humans may actually be "hard-wired" through centuries of evolution to respond positively to specific stimuli, including kindly and caring human faces, various views of nature and relaxing music (but only in certain keys).[6]

"It is clear," Ulrich said, "that the mind does matter."

How Nature Works

Ulrich's findings have been echoed by the work of others. According to Clare Cooper Marcus, MA, MCP, professor *emeritus* at the University of California Berkeley and one of the founders of the field of environmental psychology, nature is successful at reducing stress in people because it places people's minds in a state similar to that of transcendental meditation.

"When you are looking intensely at something, or you bend down to smell something, you bypass the [analytical] function of the mind,"[7] she said. You naturally stop thinking, obsessing, worrying. Your senses are awakened, which brings you into the present moment, and this has been shown to be very effective at reducing stress.

There are other benefits to working in closer harmony with nature, including increased physical exercise, an increased exposure to the healthful benefits of vitamin D derived from sunshine and the ability of natural light to counter seasonal or episodic depression.

People in unnatural environments or those who are suffering from chronic conditions enjoy even greater benefits, according to Richard Zeisel, president of Hearthstone Alzheimer Care in Lexington, Mass., a company that manages living-treatment facilities for people with the debilitating mental disease. "You can either upset people and then give them drugs to relax them, or you can *not* upset them in the first place."

Hearthstone's approach, in which gardens are an integral part of the patients' living facilities, dramatically decreases anxiety, agitation, aggression and social withdrawal among patients, thus enabling them to function with less need for antipsychotic drugs. "It's a practical

Settings such as this walkway, adorned with potted plants and flowerboxes attached to the fence, can help soothe the spirit and heal the body.

question," he said. "Would we rather spend money on drugs, or would we rather spend money on flowers?"[8]

Fooling Mother Nature

Even seniors whose environments do not include attractive views or actual gardens can get close to nature, according to horticultural therapist Teresa Hazan. She works for Legacy Health System in Portland, Ore., which provides therapy for patients at local hospitals. Hazan suggests that senior residences incorporate outdoor gardens that are accessible to everyone. Her studies show that even container gardens are enough to benefit people: a pot filled with herbs, another with a favorite shrub or tree and still others for flowers and vegetable plants. In fact, a plant in anyone's environment, she has found, can aid healing. When you become dependent on others and have less control over your life, she says, it's restorative to have something that's dependent on you. And the something that works best is nature.

Novelist Jo Clayton, a science fiction and fantasy writer with more than 30 books to her credit, found that a single amaryllis bulb helped her to climb out of the depths of depression after she was diagnosed with terminal bone cancer. "We spoke about the power of the amaryllis bulb," said Hazan, "and I compared it to the power in her."[9]

Clayton, who had never paid much attention to plants or nature before, began spending more time outdoors, eventually taking up landscape painting. Her involvement with nature, she said later, gave her the power to confront several deep-rooted family issues, which she resolved before she finally passed away.

A Testimonial to Nature

Gene Gach is convinced that his own immersion in nature has contributed to his health as well. "And my doctors have no other explanation," he said.

"Being in nature is completely different from taxes and all the worries of modern life. You have a sense of health and regeneration, a completely innocent excitement about all the life that is growing around you, and you know you are part of it.

"As a matter of fact, my only health problem is that sometimes I have trouble falling asleep. But even here the flowers help. I just repeat them, alphabetically, from memory, and I'm asleep in no time.

"*Acacia, agapanthus, aloe,* almond, *amaryllis, anemone, antherium,* apple," he recounted from memory.

"Try it! I guarantee it works."[10]

The Gardener and the Sciatica

It was three o'clock in the afternoon sometime in early October, 2007. I was putting the final touches on a book I was writing about ponds and water gardening, and my sciatic nerve, which had been bothering me increasingly for the previous few weeks, was acting up. The tingling, numbness and shooting pain down my thighs and into my legs served as a constant reminder of what this malady can do to a person's temperament: I was testier than hell.

After several hours of this, I decided to go out into the garden, near my ponds, for a few minutes to give myself a break and take my mind off my work. Three hours later, after pruning some shrubs, fixing a problem with the stream of water feeding the main pond, pulling some weeds and trimming some grass around the ivy ledge serving as a bank for a second pond, I came back inside and sat down behind my computer.

The pain was gone.

A simple coincidence.

Except that, ever since that day, I have paid particular attention to my activities when my sciatica acts up. I have studied the malady, as well, and know that simple exercise is probably the best relief for the illness, which is caused by the sciatic nerve that runs from the upper buttocks down to the feet being pinched or tweaked, possibly between two vertebrae in the lower back.

But while simple exercise certainly makes me feel better, my mental log shows that exercise done in conjunction with gardening — with being around, fooling with, feeling, smelling, tasting, touching, listening to, observing and even thinking about my gardens and koi ponds — works even better than mere physical exercise such as walking or bike-riding. As a bonus, its effects are longer lasting.

It is a remarkable combination that makes me think back to other days, to times when I was much younger, to when I was not a city dweller, to when I lived out among the woods and the wildflowers and the white-tail deer and the ruffed grouse, times of nature and of life. I think back to writing then, getting up from my desk, and going outside to tend to all matters of gardening. And when I came back inside, I felt refreshed and rejuvenated.

Like the punch-drunk boxer who has taken one too many blows to the head, I am the victim of my own worst occupational disorder — writing. And I am the beneficiary of it, as well; for, I would never have come to realize the restorative and rejuvenating powers of nature except for my writing, my malady and the research I have done in pursuit of its cure.

For this, I thank the God of Literature, whoever He/She may be. I think about Ernest Hemingway able to write only on an old

Underwood typewriter while standing up. I wonder if he, too, suffered from bouts of sciatica and, if so, if that's what kept him such an active outdoorsman. I wonder about things like that, and I look forward to repotting that fig tree that has outgrown its container in the solarium.

Gardening's Benefits

Medical journals are filled with the helpful effects of gardening upon the human soul and psyche. Whether from real reactive science or the less scientific but no less real "placebo effect," health and gardening clearly go hand in hand. Just as clear is the fact that container gardening is an effective and increasingly popular alternative to conventional gardening.

Not everyone is lucky enough to look out of the kitchen window and see a field of sunflowers waving gently in the wind. Not everyone can gaze upon an arena of waving grass ringed by butternut and shagbark hickory trees. But everyone can look out of some window and see a pot filled with heirloom tomato plants or ornamental kale or edible *Nasturtium* or even ornamental *Bougainvillaea* calling out for attention.

That's something that container gardening brings to us all. And it's one more reason to look upon growing fruits and vegetables in pots as more than the mere sum of its component parts. When you combine the healthful elements of gardening with the life-sustaining nutrients that fresh, clean fruits and vegetables bring to us, you cannot help but emerge the winner.

And that combination could well be the key to a healthful, long and fulfilling life.

01:00 IN A MINUTE

- Gardening is good physical, as well as mental, exercise.
- Numerous studies have shown that gardening can help people get and stay healthy.
- Container gardening is growing in popularity because people can grow practically anything virtually *anywhere*.

Lettuce (*Lactuca sativa*)

Habit: Leaf, head

Cultivars: Numerous cultivars are commonly grown with good success, including:

- *Green leaf:* Green Ice, Simpson Elite and Black-Seeded Simpson
- *Red leaf:* Red Sails, Lolla Rosa, Cherokee and Firecracker
- *Boston/butterhead:* Buttercrunch, Kweik, Sylvesta and Pirat
- *Head:* Ithaca, Summertime, Nevada and Tiber
- *Romaine:* Parris Island Cos, Red Romaine and Crisphead

Seed or Transplants: Both

Pot Size: Medium

Water: Water the container to maintain a uniform moisture supply during growth. Early watering will ensure that the foliage dries out before dark.

Comments: When choosing what type of lettuce to grow, remember that the darker the leaf, the richer the produce in beneficial nutrients. Most gardeners who grow lettuce raise the loose-leaf type, with either green or reddish leaves. This type is a fast-growing, long-lasting lettuce used for salads and sandwiches. Leaf lettuce basically needs only to be planted and harvested. Butterhead or Bibb lettuce is a loose-heading type with dark green leaves that are somewhat thicker than those of iceberg lettuce. Butterheads develop a light yellow, buttery appearance and are very attractive in salads. A miniature variety of butterhead, Tom Thumb, is very easy to grow and requires a short growing time. Bibb lettuce will develop bitterness if temperatures go above 95°F.

Romaine or cos is less commonly grown by gardeners but is a very nutritious lettuce that deserves attention. It too is relatively easy to grow, forming upright heads with rather wavy, attractive leaves. Crisphead, also known as iceberg, has a tightly compacted head with crisp, light-green leaves. Many gardeners find this type difficult to grow in high temperatures.

Seeds: Plant seeds to a depth approximately twice the thickness of the seed; water and tamp soil firmly. Cover pot with a clear plastic container or wrap, and wait for germination. Keep soil moist but not saturated, and keep pot out of direct sunlight to avoid overheating. Uncover at the first sign of sprouts. Thin to approximately one plant per six square inches for

Lettuce (*Lactuca sativa*)

leaf varieties and one plant per foot for head varieties. Leaf thinnings may be used in salads as soon as they are picked.

Transplants: Place in hole no deeper than original root ball, and tamp around stem firmly.

Soil: The soil should be well prepared to provide good seed-to-soil contact (when planting seed) and ensure rapid stand establishment. Maintain a soil pH between 5.8 and 6.5 for best results. Mulching is effective to control weeds and keep soil temperature cool.

Insects: Commonly encountered insects include aphids, cabbage looper, corn earworm and leafhoppers. **Solutions:** Spray for mites with biologically friendly non-detergent soap mixed with water (1T per gallon water). Slugs and snails may be picked off and disposed of by hand.

Diseases: Damping-off (a fungal condition) affects small plants, which may wilt and die soon after emergence. Other diseases include gray mold, Rhizoctonia bottom rot and Sclerotinia drop. Solutions: Use only high-quality treated seeds, and avoid excessively wet soil and prolonged exposure to cool temperatures, conditions favorable to disease.

Health Benefits: There are many types of lettuce and related greens but only one truth: The darker the leaf's color, the more nutritious it is. Beta-carotene is the chief disease-fighting element featured in dark-colored greens. As an antioxidant, it is a potent fighter against certain cancers, heart disease and cataracts. That lush dark-green color is also indicative of the presence of folic acid, which helps prevent neural-tube birth defects in the early stages of pregnancy. Researchers have also unveiled several other important contributions that folic acid has made to health. It can play a significant role in the prevention of heart disease and cellular inflammation. In fact, most salad greens (not only lettuce) offer significant sources of vitamin C, potassium and fiber. Chicory, another good source of vitamin C (a powerful antioxidant), is also linked to the prevention of heart disease, cancer and cataracts. Some other beneficial salad greens, such as arugula and watercress, are members of the cruciferous family (along with cabbage and broccoli), adding even more ammunition to the ongoing battle against disease and lending a new meaning to the phrase, "Green Revolution."

Ready for the Kitchen: Most leaf lettuce should be ready to harvest about 75 days after planting. It can be used as soon as plants are 4–6 inches tall. Bibb lettuce is mature when leaves begin to cup inward to form a loose head. Cos or Romaine is ready to use when the leaves have elongated and overlap to form a fairly tight head about 6–8 inches tall. Most head lettuce can be harvested as early as 55 days, depending on the variety. It is mature when leaves overlap to form a head similar to those available in the stores. Harvest in the morning after dew has evaporated. Regular harvests will keep leaf lettuce from bolting. Store in the refrigerator in the coolest area.

Annual Savings: Approximately $45 per year per person on average.

Gone to Pot

I don't own a garden.

I don't miss it.

I own land.

And I own plants. Lots and lots of plants. Plants everywhere. But no "garden" *per se*.

What I *do* own instead of a garden are pots. Lots and lots of pots. Expensive pots, cheap pots, pots off the shelf, pots *redux* to make them look as if they're not pots off the shelf and even homemade pots.

I own pots made out of clay and out of porcelain. I own pots made out of glass and out of plastic. I own pots made out of concrete aggregate, out of metal and out of resin. In short, if it can be shaped like a pot and made to hold water, I own it.

The reason is simple. I love pots. Or rather I love growing things in pots. The pots themselves are mostly an efficient means of preventing soil, water and plants from spilling out all over the floor.

But I don't have to worry about that. From morning to night, I am surrounded by pots, which — by and large — do a remarkably effective job of containing what they were meant to contain. That makes pots very desirable things to own. In fact, if I had my way, I would own even more.

My typical day starts off much the way yours does. I get up in the morning, have a cup of coffee and stick a plant or two into a pot. I look around for plants that have outgrown their existing containers, and I re-pot them. I see what recently acquired plants I have sitting on my planting bench, and I pot them.

I take a look at how my existing pots look in the garden, on the patio, on the deck, on the veranda and in the house. I shift them around until I think they look better. I check the soil for dryness. I water some pots and skip over others. I make a mental note of what plants need to be repotted — or what plants will need repotting in the near future — and I marvel at the lushness of the growth all around me.

I pick a fig or two. I snatch a cherry tomato. I sniff the edible *Nasturtium*. I squeeze a lime. I smile.

And then I eat breakfast.

Well, okay, maybe it's not your typical day, and maybe my pot fetish isn't normal. But it could be. And perhaps it should be.

I grow everything in pots — well, nearly everything. My living room boasts several large pots containing majestic *Ficus benjamina* trees, spiraling rubber plants, several varieties of *Dracaena*, a few types of *Philodendron*, a pot full of *sansevieria*, a bearing banana tree and some ferns.

My dining room has an eight-foot tall corn plant to one side of the table. I used to have a *Schefflera* in the far corner, but the corner is dark and, after a year, the plant began showing the strain of too little light. I moved it out into the sunroom several weeks ago, where it is recovering nicely.

That's another place I have plants, of course — the sunroom: *Dracaena marginata*, prayer plants, several Norfolk Island pines, a flowering bird of paradise, a weeping fig, a couple of tomato plants, an *Aralia*, a date palm, fresh basil, curly-leaf parsley, leaf lettuce, a ponytail palm, a couple of flowering succulents, a miniature kumquat tree, a dwarf lime tree, a few bamboo spikes and several varieties of cacti.

In short, with rare exception, I have plants growing in every room of the house.

I also have potted plants outdoors at my home here in southern Utah — lots of them. In flowerboxes, I have several varieties of sweet potato and yams, lots of herbs (sage, basil, oregano, numerous varieties of thyme, plus rosemary, chives and garlic), a couple of cape honeysuckle shrubs, flowering *Alyssum* and a few asparagus ferns.

On the patio are potted roses, rubber tree plants, tomato plants, both bulb and green onions, leaf vegetables (lettuce, spinach and edible kale), English ivy, *Aloe vera*, a few assorted ferns, some ground cover (mostly creeping Jennie and sweet woodruff), violets, *Nasturtium*, a burning bush shrub, baby tears, green and purple shamrock, Spanish daisies, numerous varieties of grass and some miscellaneous succulents. The fruits and veggies provide healthy fresh produce from mid-summer through the first frost (and sometimes beyond), while ornamentals provide a plethora of color to liven up the view from the patio chairs.

All in all, it's a great way to wake up in the morning and a fantastic way to feel revived and refreshed — walking among the planted containers.

Good Harvests from Small Packages

A process known as square-foot gardening provides encouraging news for container gardeners who enjoy growing vegetables. In effect, it says you can plant crops closer together than usually recommended with good success, so long as you provide the basic nutrients the plants require. Think of it as no-till, no-dig, no-weed gardening. Since most crop plants require only six inches of soil in depth — twice that amount for root crops — pots lend themselves ideally to vegetable gardening.

As for pot diameter, broccoli, green beans and similarly sized plants do well with one square foot of surface area (a 12-inch pot), while tomatoes, zucchini and other larger plants do best in up to three square feet. That makes vegetable gardening in pots one of the most convenient and efficient uses of soil available.

Not even ponds are exempt. In them, I have a host of water and bog plants, including cattail, water hyacinth, water lettuce, duckweed, watercress, marsh pickerel, water celery, *Cyprus* grass, *Cabomba*, horsetail and pennywort, most of which are edible.

It sounds like a lot, and I suppose it is. With all these plants growing in my household, you might think we have our hands full. Yet, the care required for all of the benefits we reap is pretty much confined to a couple hours a week spent watering and a few minutes more each day plucking off old growth and checking on the health of the plants in general.

We spend another hour a week picking produce, trimming herbs and leafy vegetables, pulling bulb crops and otherwise harvesting our rewards, mostly in late summer and fall.

We invest another hour each week dead-heading spent flower buds (removing the old flower heads stimulates new growth and more

This strawberry pot filled with—what else?—strawberry
plants requires little maintenance and spurs plants to keep
growing and bearing every spring. Note the string-like runners that produce new plants for repotting.

blooms), pruning unwanted growth and training vining plants to grow
where we want them to grow instead of where they'd prefer to grow,
which is everywhere.

Finally, we spend a good hour a week soaking in a hot tub.

For a total of about four hours' worth of work a week, then (the soaking isn't real "work"), we get to live in a veritable paradise of horticultural delights. From the most exotic faraway places in the world to some
plants that grow wild right outside our own back door, we have them all
growing in pots because we enjoy them all.

We enjoy the "work" of container gardening, too, if truth be known.
Caring for plants is a bit like caring for pets, except without all of the
drama and none of the fur balls.

Don't get me wrong. We have cats that we love to death (along with the cat mint that they enjoy grazing), and we keep our outdoor ponds stocked with koi and goldfish. But, by and large, our "babies" are our potted plants. And the work we expend in keeping them looking good, keeping them growing and healthy and flowering and producing, is just the kind of work people today don't get to enjoy often enough.

With all of these plants around, you'd think we'd be satisfied. Sure. Just about the way you'd expect Donald Trump to be happy with Trump Towers and not feel the need for more acquisitions.

The truth is that, so long as you garden — and especially when you container garden — you're going to find new plants, new species and new varieties that you're going to want to put in a pot just to have near you.

Me? I'm looking forward to the day when we have a home with enough space to allow us to grow some Japanese maple trees in pots. And perhaps a lilac shrub or two. And some more exotic fruit trees.

We currently have a few trees that are taller than I am — possibly seven or eight feet in height. But I suppose I won't really be in Hawg Heaven until I look around the house at trees spiraling skyward, two or three stories tall, smiling down at me. Perhaps a weeping mulberry or a clump of tender white birch or even a coconut palm would also be nice. It will take one mighty big house to make that happen — and substantially larger pots, I know. But somehow I can't help but think the effort would be worthwhile.

Besides, isn't dreaming part of what life is all about? And isn't container gardening just one more way to make your dreams happen?

01:00 IN A MINUTE

- If it grows *anywhere*, you can probably grow it in a pot.

- Growing fruit and vegetables in a pot is especially efficient, since it is a take-off of the "square-foot gardening" method, which relies on maximizing space and minimizing waste.

- Maintaining potted plants takes from a few minutes to a few hours each week, depending upon the number of potted plants you own.

- Dead-heading, or removing spent flower heads, will produce more vigorous plant growth and more blooms over the course of the growing season.

Cabbage (*Brassica oleracea*)

Chinese Cabbage (*Brassica rapa*, Pekinensis Group)

Habit: Head and upright

Cultivars: Numerous cultivars exist, including:

- *Cabbage:* Bravo, Market Prize, Rio Verde, Savoy Express, Tropic Giant (hybrid) and Green Jewels (hybrid)
- *Chinese cabbage:* Pak Choi Type — Joi Choi (hybrid)

Seed or transplants: Both

Pot Size: Medium

Water: Water to provide a uniform moisture supply to the crop. The container should be watered in the morning so that the foliage is dry before dark. Water sufficiently to moisten the soil to a depth of at least six inches. If gardening in pots outdoors, maintain a constant uniform moisture supply to produce a high-quality crop and to have the spring crop mature before high summer temperatures set in.

Comments: Chinese cabbage forms dense heads that may be very upright and tall (Michihili types) or round and barrel-shaped (Napa types). The leaves are slightly wrinkled and thinner than the leaves of regular cabbage with wide, crisp midribs. When choosing what type of cabbage to grow, remember that the darker green leaf and the red varieties provide more nutrition than the light green ones.

Seeds: Plant seeds to a depth approximately twice the thickness of the seed; water and tamp soil firmly. Cover pot with a clear plastic container or wrap, and wait for germination. Keep soil moist but not saturated, and keep pot out of direct sunlight to avoid overheating. Uncover at the first sign of sprouts. Thin to approximately one plant per foot for head varieties.

Transplants: Place in hole no deeper than original root ball, and tamp around stem firmly.

Soil: Cabbage (*Brassica oleracea*, Capitata Group) grows well in a wide variety of soils, but it prefers a well-drained sandy loam with high organic matter content. Soil pH should be 5.8 to 6.5.

Insects: Several worms (imported cabbageworm, cabbage looper, diamondback moth caterpillar), harlequin bugs, cabbage maggots, aphids and flea beetles are the major insect problems. **Solutions:** Pick off and destroy

Cabbage (*Brassica oleracea*)

larger worms, and spray the plant with biologically friendly non-detergent soap mixed with water (1T per gallon water) for smaller insects.

Diseases: Black rot, wire stem, damping-off, downy mildew, Alternaria leaf spot and watery soft rot are the major diseases. Cabbage is more susceptible to wire stem and downy mildew than is Chinese cabbage. Chinese cabbage is more susceptible to Alternaria. Black rot causes the most serious damage and appears as V-shaped lesions down the leaves before spreading into the water-conducting system of the plant. This disease is caused by a bacterium that is seed-borne or that can be transmitted by transplants. Warm, moist weather favors the disease. **Solutions:** Compost tea (see Chapter 15) contains organisms that attack fungal diseases and should be used as a supplement and treatment whenever possible. Otherwise, several commercially available fungicides (short-acting so as not to remain viable on the plant after harvest) are available online and at your local home and garden center. There is no control for black rot once it is established in a planting. Prevent the disease by purchasing transplants that are certified to be disease-free, or plant western-grown chemically treated seed.

Health Benefits: For the past two decades, researchers have understood the valuable role that phytonutrients play as antioxidants to disarm free radicals before they can damage human DNA cell membranes. But recently science has learned that phytonutrients in crucifers, such as cabbage, work at a much deeper level, actually signaling our genes to increase the production of enzymes designed to aid in the detoxification of harmful compounds—the ultimate body cleanser!

The phytonutrients in cruciferous vegetables initiate genes that play a complex role in placing into action dozens of detoxification enzyme partners, each balancing perfectly with the others. This natural synergy utilizes our cells' own abilities to disarm and clear free radicals and toxins from our systems. These include carcinogens, the primary reason that crucifers lower our risk of cancer more effectively than any other fruit or vegetable. In fact, studies have proven that diets rich in cruciferous vegetables create a much lower risk of prostate, colorectal and lung cancer.

In a study of more than 1,000 men conducted at the Fred Hutchinson Cancer Research Center in Seattle, WA, those eating 28 servings of miscellaneous vegetables a week showed a 35 percent lower than average risk of prostate cancer, while those consuming only three or more servings of *cruciferous* vegetables each week had a 41 percent lower prostate cancer risk.[11]

In addition to its cancer-preventive phytonutrients, cabbage is an excellent source of vitamin C, an antioxidant that helps protect cells from harmful free radicals. Cruciferous vegetables have also been beneficial in promoting women's and gastrointestinal health, as well as defending against Alzheimer's and various cardiovascular diseases.

Ready for the Kitchen: When plant is fully formed and deep in color, after approximately 90–100 days. Store in a refrigerator crisper to retain freshness.

Annual Savings: Approximately $45 per year per person on average.

Why Containers?

There are lots of reasons I prefer growing fruit and vegetables in containers over growing them in a conventional garden. For one, you can grow things in containers where you are physically unable to grow them in the ground. Lack of space, lack of light and lack of land can be difficult horticultural barriers to overcome, although I admit that I have in the past prevailed upon friends, neighbors and (especially) family members to lend me a miniscule plot of ground to furrow.

Another reason I enjoy container gardening is that I can control my plants' environments more closely in a container than I can when they are tucked into Planet Earth. Rain or no rain, acidic or alkali soil, bugs, fungus, cutworms and even poachers (whether the four- or the two-legged kind) become far less of a problem when you grow your plants in containers, particularly when they are grown indoors.

Do you live in an arid climate, such as southern California, the high desert or anywhere within a thousand miles of Las Vegas? Not to worry. It rains on your container plants every time you fill up the watering can.

Do you need to grow acid-loving plants but have access only to alkaline garden soil? A few minor corrections to the growing medium, and you'll have exactly the pH your container garden needs for healthy, productive growth.

Got bugs? Inquisitive dogs? Destructive neighbors? They are rarely a problem with container gardening, where you can place your pots indoors or out on a meticulously patrolled patio or porch in order to protect them from predators and other interlopers.

In fact, just about every advantage you can think of to growing fruit and vegetables in the ground you can achieve anywhere you like in a pot — and without most of the drawbacks to conventional gardening.

Case in point: Shortly after I married for the very first time (let's not go there, okay?), my wife and I moved to a suburban Chicago home with a large fenced yard. Naturally, the first thing I did after closing on the property was to plant several fruit trees, a few blueberry bushes (how I love blueberries!) and roses. The next week, we drove 50 miles in the dead of night to a large home in another suburb where someone had run a newspaper advertisement for a black lab puppy for sale…free!

The week after that, we were back at the nursery, replacing the blueberry shrubs and trees that the dog had dug up and left to wither and die in the hot summer sun. Ditto, the week after that. If I hadn't discovered the advantages of container gardening, we would either have run out of money or run out of dog.

In retrospect, the latter would not have been the worst idea I have ever conceived, although the beast did manage to outgrow her destructive tendencies in time, and my young son loved her dearly. Don't ask me why.

My point is that container gardening saved my sanity, saved my relationship with my son and saved me from God knows how many more trips to the nursery. (I do not give up on my fantasies easily.)

Container gardening can also provide your plants with the light they need to grow successfully. There is little frustration on earth greater than sticking a beloved stalk of living, breathing (well, sort of) tissue into the ground only to see it slowly wither and die from too little light. A lack of adequate light is one of the greatest reasons for gardening failure. I'll write more about that later.

When planting in-ground, you'll often find that the soil into which you stick your prized horticultural possession rarely receives the right amount of light for optimal growth. Even if the light is sufficiently strong to satisfy the plant's need for life, it may not be strong enough to induce the plant to produce flowers or, more so, to set fruit and carry that fruit through to harvest.

The opposite can also be true. If you plant a shade-loving low-light plant such as lettuce or spinach into a plot of outdoor ground in full sunlight, you run the risk of burning it out and killing it.

Container plants, though, can be moved around to the best possible location to take advantage of the light for maximum growth and sustained health. I know some container gardeners (not me — I'm nowhere near ambitious enough for this) who set their light-loving plants in an eastern exposure to take advantage of the early morning sun and move them to the opposite end of the house as the light source shifts steadily toward the west.

Some people call that dedication. I call it fanatic. Whatever you call it, the point is that you have the *option* of placing container plants into a far greater array of lighting conditions than you would have by sticking your plants into holes in the middle of your backyard.

Fortunately, there are several simpler and more effective ways of giving your potted plants exactly the light they need for best possible growth than playing "follow the sun," as some of my gardener friends do. We'll talk more about those options later.

In the end, container gardening gives you lots of advantages over in-ground gardening with very few of the disadvantages.

To the Rescue

I live in the desert. Actually, I live in a house, and the house lives in the desert. Nevertheless, I buy plants that I enjoy having around me. Over the years, I have found that some of these plants have failed to return the favor. In particular, I can name several dozen specimens of *Begonia*, Swedish ivy (*Plectranthus australis*) and cucumber that I have tried and failed miserably to acclimate to my surroundings.

The only possible reason for their lack of reciprocation to all my best gardening efforts: an inhospitable environment. Namely, too much heat and not enough humidity.

By growing these and other species indoors in containers, I finally found success. Container gardening allows me to control the environment of these plants, including light, water, humidity and temperature, while enabling me to enjoy their beauty. As a bonus, the fruit and vegetables they provide me are mighty tasty!

D.J. Herda

Aloe vera is one of the easiest and healthiest plants to grow in containers, indoors or out! As a bonus, it's great for aiding burns and digestive problems, which puts it right at home in the kitchen.

Naturally, not everything in life is a sure thing, and the same holds true for container gardening. Over-watering — rarely a problem with plants in the Great Outdoors — can be a serious problem with container plants, particularly with plants kept in the house. Conversely, under-watering can take its toll on container plants, too, most often with potted plants kept outdoors.

But, with a little common sense, some sound advice and a bit of practical experience, you'll soon get the hang of growing plants in containers, and growing everything from bearing trees and shrubs to small fruit, vegetables and even edible cactus and succulents such as *Aloe vera* will become as easy as falling off a manure truck.

Oh, and that's one more advantage to container gardening: you can add just the right amount and type of nutrients to your potting mixture to help keep your plants looking and growing their best, something that is often more difficult to do with in-ground plantings.

If none of this has yet convinced you that container gardening is your own personal wave of the future, that it is both economically sound and theoretically practical, that you can grow better, healthier, more attractive edible plants in containers than you can grow conventionally, here's one last thought:

Plant a tree in the ground, and that's where it stays. Plant one in a container, and it's there for as long as you want it to be — no more, no less. You can change plants with the seasons, move your containers from one room to another, reposition plants within a room, stagger your plantings for a continuous harvest, set the plants outside in the summer and bring them inside during the cold days of winter, arrange them in groups and even combine multiple plants in a single container.

You can change color schemes to match your home's furnishings, add texture and drama to your home's design palette and create specific moods to meet your needs, all with a degree of flexibility unknown to conventional gardeners. And you can do all that while saving a ton of money on your grocery bill.

That's one of the most attractive features of container gardening.

01:00 IN A MINUTE

- Container gardening is an efficient way of growing plants regardless of where you live.

- You can control your potted plant's environment far more easily than you can with plants tucked into the ground.

- Growing plants in pots is not foolproof, but it comes as close as anything science has yet devised.

Peas (*Pisum sativum*)

Habit: Bush and trellis

Cultivars: Some suggested garden pea cultivars are:
- Little Marvel, Thomas Laxton, Wando, Freezonian, Frosty, Knight, Alderman (tall-growing), Sparkle and Green Arrow

Seed or Transplants: Both

Pot Size: Medium

Water: Water moderately to a soil depth of at least six inches, allowing soil to dry out between waterings.

Comments: When choosing what type of peas to grow, remember that vining or trellis varieties can quickly take over a space. In addition, they need something on which to crawl—a stake, trellis, open-weave curtain or even a nearby bookshelf—which may prove to be less than ideal. Bush varieties, on the other hand, are far more compact and therefore better suited for growing in pots.

Seeds: Plant seeds to a depth approximately twice the thickness of the seed; water and tamp soil firmly. Cover pot with a clear plastic container or wrap, and wait for germination. Keep soil moist but not saturated, and keep pot out of direct sunlight to avoid overheating. Uncover at the first sign of sprouts. Thin to approximately one plant per six inches for vining varieties or one plant per foot for bush varieties.

Peas (*Pisum sativum*)

Mike Hillis

Transplants: Place in hole no deeper than original root ball, and tamp around stem firmly.

Soil: Peas can be grown in a wide variety of soils, but good drainage is essential. Peas do best in a pH of 6.0 to 6.7.

Insects: Watch for aphids, leafhoppers and whiteflies, particularly if plants are kept outdoors. **Solutions:** Spray for insects with biologically friendly non-detergent soap mixed with water (1T per gallon water).

Diseases: Root rot, a fungus that lives in the soil, is a constant threat, especially to young plants. Also, powdery mildew and wilt can attack peas. **Solutions:** As a means of containing contamination, never plant peas in the previous year's potting soil to reduce the incidence of soil-borne diseases that can build up over time.

Use only sterilized soil or potting mix and, if necessary, drench with one gallon of water mixed with six drops of tea tree oil, which has strong antibacterial and anti-fungal properties. Compost tea (see Chapter 15) contains organisms that attack fungus and should be used as both a supplement and treatment whenever possible.

Health Benefits: Green peas provide numerous nutrients, including vitamin C, which are instrumental in helping to prevent the development of cancer. A high intake of vitamin C has been shown to reduce the risks for virtually all forms of cancer, including leukemia, lymphoma and lung, colorectal and pancreatic cancers as well as sex-hormone–related cancers such as breast, prostate, cervix and ovarian cancers. Vitamin C is the body's first and most effective line of antioxidant protection, helping to prevent damage to DNA while aiding the body in dealing with various environmental pollutants and toxic chemicals. It is also beneficial in enhancing the body's immune system and inhibiting the formation of cancer-causing compounds such as nitrosamines, chemicals that the body produces after digesting processed meats containing nitrates.

Ready for the Kitchen: When pea pods are fully formed and beginning to swell, usually around 60–70 days after germination . Pick the pods off the plant, allowing the plant to continue producing peas throughout the growing season.

Annual Savings: Approximately $34 per year per person on average.

Dressed for Success

Just as you look terrific when you go out for a night on the town (or even a day at the office), dressed in that dynamite outfit you just know makes you look absolutely irresistible, plants look better dressed up, too. But for a plant, the best designer ware you can get is a flower pot, box or other container to show it off.

Sure, you can stick a plant in any old plastic throwaway you pick up behind the nursery, but why bother dressing down your plants when good-looking and even *great*-looking pots are relatively inexpensive and available nearly everywhere — including, I'm betting, right inside your own home.

If you've been gardening for as long as I have, you probably have dozens of spare planters around the house. If you don't, don't despair. You can go out to the local antique store or home decorating shop and pick up something really nice for a couple hundred dollars. Or you can get by for a buck or two by simply shopping around, remaining flexible and being a bit creative. Before you begin snooping around for that pot to die for, though, take a few minutes to think about what type of container will be best for your plants.

Plants like plenty of "leg room." They need room to grow, both above ground and below. In general, a plant's root system should be at least one-half the height of the plant at the plant's maturity. If a plant grows to twelve inches in height, then, you're going to want a pot that provides you with at least six inches of root room.

Note that I'm *not* talking about a pot that's six inches deep, here. You can't expect to fill a six-inch pot with soil to the brim and not make a mess every time you go to water. You'll need to allow at least half an inch of extra depth, and preferably an inch, to make sure that the water doesn't run over the sides of the container and out across the floor.

Also, remember that root crops, where the edible portion of the plant grows beneath the surface of the soil, are going to require even more depth to account for the size of the root. In such cases, it's wise to have a pot as deep as the root at maturity plus four inches. A beet root that is likely to be four inches tall, then, should be grown in a pot that allows for eight inches of depth.

Avoid *at all costs* the notion that when you buy a plant at the local garden center or nursery you can keep it in the same pot after you get it home. Plants are grown by commercial nurseries in small pots for a purpose. The cramped growing conditions force the plant to produce more roots in a concentrated area, resulting in healthier looking top growth. That, in turn, appeals to consumers such as you and me.

These plants do well in such small containers because nurseries feed and water them nearly continually to keep them alive and prospering — up to the point that you take it home. Then get ready for trouble. Unless you're equipped to feed and water your root-bound plants daily (and sometimes more often than that), you're going to want to transplant the little critters into something roomier, with more soil to hold more crucial water and nutrients.

Likewise, if you buy a new container into which to transplant your new acquisition, make sure that the pot isn't merely an inch or two larger than the original container. Choose a pot that's roomy enough to hold the plant at maturity. In that way, you won't have to transplant more than once.

This is especially important with food crops. It's one thing to keep an ornamental plant looking fairly healthy in a relatively small pot. But fruits and vegetables need extra room — and the additional nutrients — that larger pots afford them in order to flower and set fruit.

How will you know how big a plant will grow when it's mature? Check the tags on the plants or pots where you purchase them. If that doesn't give you the answer, do a little Internet research. (You'll find some great free plant information resources in the appendix of this book.) Taking the time to match the size of the pot to the size of the mature plant will help you enjoy greater container gardening success.

Shopping Around for the Right Containers

When you set out to find the right containers for your plants, the first place to look is where you buy your plants. It makes sense. Why make three or four trips to different stores when you can buy everything you need in one place?

But don't feel intimidated into buying something you don't like — or something that costs more than you're willing to spend — just because it's readily available. Often, taking the time to shop around, checking out various nurseries, home centers, discount shops, other retail outlets and the Internet is the most economical way to purchase pots.

And don't forget to watch for seasonal specials. I love to shop for pots in the fall because of all the sales. That's the best time of year to get a great deal on even the most costly designer pots because stores start getting nervous about carrying over their summer stock round about the first of October. You can often find some really great bargains at that time of year.

Even if you're not planning on using a sale pot immediately, having it on hand for the future is a great way to be prepared while saving big bucks.

You can also find great deals on pots at yard and garage sales, community sales, rummage sales and auctions. People place relatively little personal value on pots once they've been used. But in my experience, even the grungiest-looking pots will clean up quite nicely once you get them home.

I've been fortunate enough to find pots that would easily cost more than a hundred dollars retail for only a few dollars at a sale. You get to pocket the change while showing off all those costly pots to friends and neighbors without anyone being the wiser.

Remember to remain flexible, and keep your eyes open. Sometimes stores that you would least expect will receive a shipment of pots, stores that otherwise rarely carry any plant paraphernalia at all. I have found great deals on pots in grocery stores, antique shops and

Three of the author's favorite decorator pots, purchased during the off-season for less than US$7 apiece.

second-hand and consignment shops. These might not be among the first places you would think to shop for your pots, but you should keep them in mind as you make your rounds.

Adapting Containers to Your Needs

There's another way to get great-looking pots for little or no money. It's a trick I have often used, especially when acquiring large pots (which can be very costly — the bigger the pot, the larger the tab). Pick up an inexpensive pot made from plastic, tin or whatever other suitable material you find and dress it up by placing it inside a wicker basket or some other type of decorative receptacle. For only a few dollars, you can often create the illusion of having a unique and costly planter while providing your plants with plenty of leg room to grow.

Just be certain when placing a pot inside any porous vessel, such as a wicker basket, to put a saucer under the plant inside the basket. In that way, when the excess water drains from the soil, as it inevitably will, it won't run all over the house.

Check inside the basket from time to time to make sure the pot isn't sitting in a saucer full of water, though. Sometimes out of sight really is out of mind, and most plants don't do well with continuously wet feet.

To remove standing water from a saucer inside a decorative container, either lift the pot out and empty the saucer before replacing the plant or, if the plant is too large or bulky to lift, place some towels or old rags next to the basket and tilt it until the excess water runs out. As an alternative, if you have room to reach down to the saucer, you can soak up the excess water with an absorbent cloth or sponge.

If you find yourself regularly emptying saucers or water, cut back on the amount of water you give your plants to alleviate the problem in the future. There is a thin line between giving your plant just the amount of water it needs and giving it too much or too little. By adjusting your watering routine, you'll eliminate the need to run around the house, tilting plants and emptying saucers for the rest of your life.

Another inexpensive way to match a pot to your tastes, as well as to your home décor, is to decorate the pot's exterior. You can pick up an affordable clay pot, for instance, and use spray paint to change its color. You can also decorate it with stencil (patterns are available at most paint stores and craft shops). Lacquer over the stencils, once the paint has dried, to protect them from the elements.

I have also upgraded the look of an ordinary inexpensive pot by gluing slats of wood to the outside, running the slats vertically from top to bottom. The results are terrific, and you can stain or paint the wood to better match the surroundings. Leave a small space between each of the slats to provide an added element of depth and texture to the finished product.

You might also consider wrapping an old or ugly pot with twine or rope to give it a decorator look. Use small dabs of glue or silicon calk periodically to help keep the rope in place and prevent it from slipping down or stretching out with exposure to the elements.

Just remember: Whenever using glue on a porous pot, such as clay, choose a non-soluble cement, such as silicon calk, quick-drying epoxy or instant-glue. Otherwise, every time you water, the pot will bleed moisture through to the outside and slowly decay the glue.

About Clay Pots

Clay pots are among the oldest pots in history. Once used by ancestral human beings to cook in and eat from, they are now manufactured by the tens of thousands, making them inexpensive and, thus, immensely popular pots for container gardening.

Ah, but while clay pots are good all-around containers for most plants, they do tend to leach moisture into the air, which means they suck the moisture from the soil inside the pots, drying the soil out more quickly than is the case in less porous pots, such as those made from plastic or glazed ceramic. If you use clay pots, be certain to check for soil moisture more frequently than with other types of pots.

Also, since clay pots filled with moistened soil are extremely heavy, be sure that you use them only in areas where they don't need to be moved frequently — especially true with very large, tree-sized pots. It's also a good idea to place all large potted plants on trivets fitted with casters for when you absolutely must move them.

Another elegant way of dressing up inexpensive pots is to decorate them with broken shards of colorful ceramic or glass tile or pebbles. Simply trowel the appropriate tile cement onto the outside of the pot and place the shards or stones wherever you want them. Once the entire project has dried, grout the seams between the pieces and allow the grout to dry thoroughly before protecting the grout with an appropriate sealer. You can get more advice and supplies from the flooring department of your local home center or online.

If you decide to try this decorator trick, don't be timid. Be creative. Break up the tile into small pieces with a hammer (be sure to wear goggles to protect your eyes from flying debris), and vary the color and sizes of the tiles to suit your tastes and design palette.

Once your project is complete, you can coat the entire exterior of your newly created designer pot with clear acrylic or any one of a number of other suitable sealants to keep dirt and other debris from dulling the finish.

If You Build It, They Will Grow

Yet another inexpensive way to get a very expensive pot for next to no cost is to build it yourself from scratch. Depending upon just how handy you happen to be, you can use nearly any medium that's capable of holding water — including wood (although you will need to take some additional steps when using porous material).

If you're handy with a hammer and a saw, you can build a square or rectangular planter to nearly any size you desire. Once your project is complete, use a waterproofing compound, such as epoxy or waterproof paint, to coat the interior. Test the pot when the compound has fully dried by filling it with water and setting it outside or indoors in the sink or bathtub. If the outside is still dry 24 hours later, you can be pretty confident that you're ready to plant in it.

As an alternative to using a waterproof sealant, you can line the pot with a heavy grade of plastic or vinyl. Keep the sheeting in place by using a small dab of silicon calk wherever needed.

After finishing your container project, make sure to drill quarter-inch drainage holes every four inches or so in the bottom, and set a saucer slightly smaller in diameter than the pot (so it can't be seen) beneath it. Lift the pot off the saucer periodically to empty out any standing water, which might eventually reach the lip of the saucer and overflow, ruining your flooring.

You can use a similar technique to make custom-built window boxes for the exterior of your home (or even the interior, if you're creative and have lots of window space). With a little basic woodworking knowledge, you'll find building a window box relatively simple — about a "two" on a scale of difficulty from one to five. For outdoor window boxes, use a water-retardant species of wood such as

These two rectangular containers constructed of common-grade cedar were made to sit on the rear wall of a pond. The insides were sealed with waterproof paint, and drain holes were drilled in the back to prevent excess water from draining into the pond.

cedar or redwood. Be sure to use galvanized nails or screws to hold your window box together unless you don't mind those black "weep marks" that come from using untreated metal fasteners.

Of course, there are many other materials besides wood from which you can build a container unique to your personal tastes and environment. Spend an hour or so wandering around your local home supply center, and I guarantee you'll find more than you ever knew existed. You can use virtually any material that can be forged into a vessel shape to hold your plant — from Plexiglas and plastic to corrugated metal (great for that ultra-modern industrial look), PVC pipe and even spray foam (the kind that comes in a can).

Remember, though, that once your project is complete, you'll need to test it for water tightness — especially if the container will be located indoors — to make certain you don't end up ruining a beautiful carpet, table or hardwood floor.

Wild and Crazy Guy

There's yet another way to secure a large and wildly diverse group of containers to hold your fruits and vegetables. You can "appropriate" them. No, I'm not talking about stealing them from beneath your neighbor's back porch. That would be unprincipled, not to mention illegal! I'm talking about adapting and adopting.

Do you have anything around the house that is sufficient in size to hold some potting mix and a plant or two? Here are a couple of things I discovered around my house while writing this chapter.

An old hiking boot

A wastepaper basket

A discarded file box

A large wooden salad bowl

A cardboard box

A discarded lamp shade

A plastic milk jug

A desk drawer

A deep wicker serving tray

A large vegetable juice can

I know what you're thinking. Too much sun, not enough selenium.

Actually, I've been getting just the right amount of each, thank you. No, there's nothing wrong with me upstairs — at least, nothing more than usual. But here's my point. If it's large enough to hold a plant, it's suitable for a planter.

Of course, if the object is water-tight, such as a plastic milk jug or a juice can, you're already one step ahead of the pack. You can fill it with potting mix, plant whatever you want in it, and sit back to await the fruits of your labor.

If the object is anything but water-tight, such as a cardboard box or a shoe, you're going to have to waterproof it before turning it into a planter.

You can do that either by painting the object, inside and out, with a waterproof paint or epoxy, or you can do something that's far simpler and less costly: line it with plastic.

Avoid using an inexpensive grade of plastic, such as plastic food wrap, a trash bag or a flimsy two-for-a-dollar drop cloth, because if it punctures (and thin plastic always punctures), you're going to rue the day you ever bought this book.

The plastic you'll need to use is at least three millimeters in thickness, available in different-sized rolls at most home centers, nurseries and hardware stores. For an even sturdier piece of goods — something that will last a lifetime — use vinyl pond liner, which you can get online or at many home and nursery centers.

Whichever vinyl product you use, before you line your new planter, use a light coating of silicon calk to cover the inside bottom. Squeeze a dollop out of the tube and, using an old paint brush, a spoon or your fingertips (put on a pair of disposable gloves first!), cover the entire bottom of the planter. While the silicon is still wet, cut an overly large piece of vinyl from the role, stuff it inside the planter and press it into contact with the silicon. Allow to dry for one or two days.

Next, drill weep holes every four inches or so to drain any excess water from your planter. Once that's complete, you can fill your planter. Start with a coarse layer of stones or gravel and add potting mix nearly to the top. Press the mixture in firmly to push the vinyl lining flush against the planter's inside walls.

Finally, cut the excess vinyl so that it's half an inch or so below the neck of the vessel and secure it to the vessel with a thin bead of silicon.

The results? A brand new (well, *recycled* new) container ready to take its place in your "garden."

If you want to use your newly lined recycled planter indoors, make sure to place some sort of inexpensive saucer or tray beneath the drainage holes to prevent water from running all over the house.

The Shape of the Future

Whether you decided to buy your pots, build them from scratch or reconstitute them from recycled materials, you should never be at a lack of containers for your garden. From those three sources alone, you'll have access to a huge selection of sizes and shapes — cylindrical, conical, rounded and square. Still others are "indeterminate" (shoe-shaped?).

The shape of the pots you choose won't necessarily matter much to the plants you grow in them, so long as you keep in mind that the pot should allow for ample root growth and adequate drainage. Be sure that the top, or neck, of the container is wide enough, of course, to accommodate the plant (and wide enough to transplant it later, as will likely be necessary if you plan on growing a large perennial plant over the course of several years). A wide neck also has the advantage of being easier to water without spilling, and it offers more opportunity for oxygen exchange — allowing the discharge of carbon dioxide during the day while taking in oxygen, and just the reverse at night — which is critical to stimulate healthy plant growth.

About the worst mistake I ever made in choosing a shape for a planter was selecting an expensive egg-shaped designer pot. It had a wide middle and a narrow neck. I planted a perennial tree inside the pot. When it eventually outgrew its home, I set about removing it for transplanting into something larger.

Imagine my overwhelming joy when, only seconds into a project that should have taken no more than a minute or two, I realized that the root mass was three times larger than the pot's opening.

In order to prevent losing all of those delicate life-sustaining roots by yanking the plant out by the stem (which could *also* damage the stem), I finally ended up using a power saw to cut the pot in two. I was amazed at how the root ball had filled up every cubic inch of soil inside the container. No wonder I couldn't coax the plant loose!

All was not lost, however. Once I'd finished repotting the plant into a more conventional container, I was able to use some quick-drying cement to rejoin the two halves again. After a little sanding and a fresh coat of paint, it looked as good as new.

Now I plant only annuals in it, so that at the end of each growing season, I can rip them out without worry.

A lesson learned.

01:00   IN A MINUTE

- Give plants plenty of "leg room."

- Shop around for the best prices on pots.

- If you can't find what you want at the price you can afford, decorate or build it yourself from scratch.

- Pay attention to the shape of your pots: shallow containers are ideal for herbs and low-growing plants such as strawberries; short, fat, dumpy containers are great for tall plants; containers that have a narrow collar are going to prove a problem for repotting.

- If you're in a whimsical or frugal mood, you can recycle nearly any container into an effective and attractive planter

Snap Beans (*Phaseolus vulgaris*)

Habit: Pole, bush and half-runner

Cultivars: Recommended for container gardening:
- *Bush type:* Bush Blue Lake 274, Derby, Provider, Resistant Cherokee Wax, Roma II, Tendercrop and Venture
- *Pole type:* Blue Lake, Kentucky Blue, Kentucky Wonder, Kentucky Wonder 191 and Kwintus (Early Riser)
- *Half-runner type:* Mountaineer White

Seed or Transplants: Both

Pot Size: Medium

Water: Water moderately, to a depth of about six inches. Light sprinkles will encourage shallow rooting of the plants. The critical period for moisture is during pod set and pod development. Morning watering is best so that the leaves dry out before evening, discouraging fungal diseases.

Comments: Beans do best in full sun or bright indirect light with uniform fertilizing and watering during their growth cycle. Pole beans are going to require a trellis or other support on which to grow, making them somewhat awkward for growing indoors, particularly because some varieties are capable of growing quite "long." Bush beans are much more compact and more suitable in general for container gardening. Once the beans begin forming, the plant bears throughout much of the season.

Seeds: Plant seeds to a depth approximately twice the thickness of the seed; water; and tamp soil firmly with your fingers. Cover pot with a clear plastic container or wrap, and wait for germination. Keep soil moist but not saturated, and keep pot out of direct sunlight to avoid overheating. Uncover at the first sign of sprouts. When three sets of leaf axils form, thin to approximately one plant per six inches.

Snap Beans (*Phaseolus vulgaris*)

Transplants: Place in hole no deeper than original root ball and tamp around stem firmly.

Soil: Snap beans require moderate amounts of fertilizer and a pH between 5.8 and 6.5 for optimal fertility levels.

Insects: Insect problems may include Mexican bean beetles, thrips, aphids, corn earworms and stink bugs. **Solutions:** Spray for insects with biologically friendly non-detergent soap mixed with water (1T per gallon water).

Diseases: Common diseases include root rot, rust and gray mold. **Solutions:** Choose resistant varieties and keep misting and moisture in general to a minimum. To contain existing disease, try Horseradish Fungicide. (See Chapter 15.)

Health Benefits: Beans are an excellent source of vitamins C and K plus manganese. They are also high in vitamin A (mostly via their concentration of carotenoids, including beta-carotene), dietary fiber, potassium, folate and iron. As if that weren't enough, they are an efficient source of magnesium, thiamin, riboflavin, copper, calcium, phosphorous, protein, omega-3 fatty acids and niacin. They are, in short, a health food store in a pot.

The vitamin K in green beans is critical for maintaining strong bones. Vitamin K1 helps to prevent the formation of osteoclasts, which causes cells within bones to break down. As a bonus, the beneficial bacteria in our intestines convert some K1 into K2, which activates osteocalcin, the major non-collagen protein contained in bone. Osteocalcin anchors calcium molecules inside of the bone, creating a stronger, more durable skeletal structure.

Green beans are also beneficial in providing nutrients to fight atherosclerosis and diabetic heart disease. Their vitamins A and C work to reduce the number of free radicals in the body. Vitamin C, a water-soluble antioxidant, and the beta-carotene in Vitamin A, a fat-soluble antioxidant, work in combination to prevent cholesterol from becoming oxidized. Oxidized cholesterol is more likely to stick to the blood vessel walls, creating blockages that can lead to heart attack or stroke.[12]

Green beans are also beneficial in reducing inflammation of the cells, promoting overall colon health and providing a rich source of iron.

Ready for the Kitchen: May be harvested as soon as bean pods are swollen and ripe, although they may also be left on the plant to harden into dried beans long after the plant itself dies off. Full maturation is typically 50–60 days from seed.

Annual Savings: Approximately $38 per year per person on average.

Matching Your Plants to Their Containers

One of the greatest advantages to growing plants in containers is the ability to bring the specific requirements of each plant right to its front porch, both quickly and easily. You can adjust the potting mixture, change the soil pH, alter the nutrient content and level and modify the lighting to satisfy each individual plant's specific needs. As a bonus, you don't have any back-breaking digging and painstaking weeding. Of course, you *will* need to water your container plants regularly, but that's a requirement you would face even with most in-ground gardens.

Most vegetables you're going to grow in containers will be annuals, so you're going to have to replant at least once a season to keep a healthy harvest going, from spring to fall. Many fruits, on the other hand, grow on shrubs and trees and will thus be perennial in nature. Even strawberries are perennials. That means they'll be around year after year to provide you with an attractive foliar display, as well as a regular harvest of tasty and nutritious produce.

But before you can start salivating over your first harvest, you're going to have to follow the rules. And one of the first rules of thumb in container gardening is selecting the best container for your plants. That means you have to select the right size and shape of container for the size and growing habit of the plants you're going to be growing.

Match Container Size to Plants

Some plants, such as tomatoes, can grow pretty large — both above and below ground — and will require a suitably large container to house them. Others, such as peppers, are much more compact in their growth habit and require smaller pots overall.

Some root crops, such as radishes, carrots and beets, are going to need deeper containers than many other plants in order for the produce to form properly. If you crowd a root crop, the results are going to be stunted, twisted or possibly even nonexistent harvests.

Some fruit crops, such as dwarf peach and plum trees, are going to need large containers in order to satisfy their needs as heavy feeders. If you don't keep sufficient nutrients available to nurture the plant, the plant will struggle merely to stay alive, and you'll wind up with a very poor fruit crop.

That doesn't mean you can't grow large plants in small containers and vice versa; but doing so is going to be much more difficult — and with much less desirable results — than matching the two properly.

Also, a large plant in a small container is going to use up all the water and nutrients in short order, and you'll find yourself constantly running for the watering can and fertilizer just to keep the plant alive and limping along.

A small plant in a large container, on the other hand, may not look very nice and is certainly not very efficient use of space.

It makes sense, then, to get to know as much as possible about your plant's growing habits before matching a plant to a pot.

Over-wintering Container Plants

The main issue with having container-grown potted plants outside all year long is their hardiness (tolerance to high summer temperatures and low winter temperatures). If your plants can't take the scorching summer sun and heat where you live, you'll have to bring them indoors or move them to a shadier outdoor location during the hottest part of the day. If they can't take the average cold temperatures of winter, you have two options: bring them indoors during winter or insulate the containers with foam, Styrofoam, fiberglass batting or a similar product.

Remember that, because containers are above ground, the container temperature will get much colder than the ground temperature. In fact, the soil in a container is usually the same as the ambient, or air, temperature. If it's 10°F outside, you can bet the soil in your container is just about the same. While the plant's shoots (the above-ground growth) might be able to tolerate such cold temperatures, its roots, which are its most vulnerable part, may not.

You can sometimes defeat Mother Nature by choosing plant cultivars designed to do well in colder climes (select a species that is two USDA hardiness zones lower than the zone in which you live). You can also over-winter container plants in protected areas, such as a garage, unheated basement or other structure that is cold but not below freezing (32°F or 0°C).

For delicate annuals, tender perennials and tropical plants ill suited to low-temperature exposure, you'll have to bring the plants indoors during winter and place them in a high-light location.

Remember, too, that terra cotta containers and other such porous materials exposed to freezing conditions will likely crack during the freezing-and-thawing cycle; so if you live in a cold climate and want your prized pots to last longer than a season or two, choose materials such as fiberglass, plastic or wood, or bring your natural containers indoors to avoid the ravages of freezing and thawing.

Some Considerations When Choosing

Pot size isn't the only consideration you'll be faced with when matching your pots to your plants or vice versa. Here are a few more things to contemplate.

Container Scale: Scale is the relationship of the pot to its surroundings, as well as to the plants you place inside the pot. For a pleasing visual effect, your plants should be in proportion to the size of the container. Picture a fully grown tomato plant in a pot the size of a can of mushroom soup. The scale would be entirely wrong, and the scene would look ridiculous. Conversely, a pea plant in a 24-inch pot would appear absolutely preposterous.

In order to achieve a more pleasing appearance, the plant should be approximately one-third to one-half the size of the container holding it.

A plant that takes up a cubic foot of space ($1' \times 1' \times 1'$), then, should be in a pot at least twice that size and as large as three times that size, or two to three cubic feet.

Remember to take into consideration the potted plant's surroundings within the home environment. Don't place a solitary 10-inch pot in the corner of a two-story solarium, or it will look a bit like a gnat on a hog's, uhh, behind — absolutely ridiculous. Keep single pots and smaller pots confined to smaller areas within the home, or move them to the deck or patio.

Container Color: The color of your containers should complement their surroundings. Choose a natural color that blends well with your décor indoors. Brightly colored pots — red, blue and yellow, for example — do best as featured elements surrounded by other less vibrant pots. The eye will fall first on the splashy pot and gradually take in the other elements. Remember that the plant should be the focus of attention; don't force it to compete for attention with the pot.

For the least intrusive pots, choose natural, unglazed terra cotta containers or pots in a muted earth tone.

Container Grouping: Pay attention to the number of pots you have in any given area. A single pot set off all alone nearly always looks inconse-

Containers come in all sorts of sizes, shapes and degrees of whimsy. Make sure the container you choose fits the growing habits of the plant for which it's intended.

quential or lost, stark by comparison to its surroundings. By grouping three or more pots together, you'll lend a more natural look to the area. (An uneven number, interestingly, appears to the eye to be more natural than an even number, which the brain conceives to be contrived or staged — you remember: *Star Trek.*)

In order not to appear too garish, avoid grouping pots of wildly varying colors, shapes and sizes together. One large terra cotta pot surrounded by two smaller pots of similar construction, for instance, would be ideal for most corners, atriums or entryways to a home.

As you would with any decorator elements, group pots according to their size, placing the larger pots toward the rear of the grouping and the smaller pots toward the front and off to the sides.

Container Style and Shape: Choose a container that suits the general style of your home or garden or the area where the container is to be placed. Is the style of your home country casual? Select a pot that complements it. Is the pot to go into a room adorned with Oriental artifacts? A Far Eastern motif would work best. Is your home classically formal in its décor? A Grecian urn-style pot or something similarly ornate might work best.

Just remember, when selecting a pot with a sculpted profile, to avoid choosing impractical pots with narrow necks, for example, which could make repotting difficult.

Container Drainage: All pots must allow for adequate drainage. Otherwise, the plant's roots will end up sitting in water; oxygen will be unable to reach the delicate feeder roots; and the plant will drown.

If you are determined to use a decorative container with no drainage holes (on a carpet or hardwood floor, for example), set the plant in a well-ventilated pot only slightly smaller than the decorative container; then place some pebbles inside the decorative container, and place the potted plant on the pebbles. Then, whenever you water, the excess will drain out of the plant's container and into the decorative pot.

Remember to empty the decorative container of accumulated water, though, to prevent the level from building up to a point where the inner pot is sitting in a stagnant pool slowly feeding death upward through the soil to the plant's roots.

Container Material: The material from which the pot is made influences not only the aesthetic appeal of the planting but also the rigor with which your plants will grow. Common terra cotta, clay or cement pots, for example, are porous, allowing the soil to dry out more rapidly; so watering must be done more frequently than when using a nonporous container made of plastic, metal or resin or one that has a ceramic coating, which will require less watering.

Whatever size and style pots you choose, remember to match the planting to its environment. Pots and plants should work together aesthetically instead of fighting one another, and the planted container should fit comfortably into its environment, whether indoors or out.

Oh, and one more thing. If you have cats, be prepared. Cats *love* potted plants. To them, they are the most natural litter boxes in the world.

To discourage your cats from digging around (and worse) in your large pots, cover the surface with crumpled aluminum foil (for a short-term deterrent), large stones (large enough so that the cats can't move them out of the way when they want to urinate) or pine cones (which look great and can be left in place year-round).

01:00 IN A MINUTE

- Match container size to the size of your plants at maturity in order to provide for best growth and most pleasing aesthetic effect.

- Bring naturally porous planters (terra cotta, concrete, etc.) indoors to protect from cold winter temperatures and possible cracking.

- Take into consideration the color, style, shape and construction material when selecting the best container for your plants.

- Group your containers for greatest efficiency and aesthetic appeal.

Cucumber (*Cucumis sativus*)

Habit: Vine, bush

Cultivars: Burpless cucumbers (appropriately named, I assure you) are long and slender with a tender skin. Bush varieties produce well in a limited amount of space and are a good alternative for con-

tainer gardening. New varieties are being released that are
advertised as all-female, or
gynoecious, types. These plants
tend to bear fruit earlier with a
more concentrated fruit set and
better yield, because they have
either a greater proportion of
female flowers to male flowers
or female flowers only. It is the

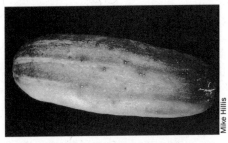

Cucumber (*Cucumis sativus*)

female flowers that turn into fruit. Popular cultivars include:

- *Slicers:* Salad Bush (hybrid), Straight Eight, Sweet Slice, Sweet Suc-
  cess (hybrid), Burpless (hybrid) and Poinsett 76
- *Picklers:* Fancipak (hybrid), Calypso, Carolina, County Fair, Homemade
  Pickles and Regal

Seed or Transplants: Both

Pot Size: Medium to large

Water: Water the container frequently to maintain a uniform moisture
supply during growth. Early watering will ensure that the foliage dries out
before dark.

Comments: Fruit is produced only when insects carry pollen to a female
cucumber flower, and honeybees are essential for this purpose, so cucumbers should be grown outdoors at least until fruit is set. The first 10–20
flowers on a plant are male and will not produce fruit. Bitterness results
from temperature variations of more than 20°F or from storing cucumbers
too near other ripening vegetables. Because cucumber plants are very tender and can be killed by even light frost, overnight your plants indoors when
temperatures fall.

Seeds: Plant seeds to a depth approximately twice the thickness of the
seed; water and tamp soil firmly. Cover pot with a clear plastic container
or wrap, and wait for germination. Keep soil moist but not saturated, and
keep pot out of direct sunlight to avoid overheating. Uncover at the first
sign of sprouts. Thin to approximately one plant per six square inches.
Transplants: Place in hole no deeper than the original root ball, and tamp
around stem firmly with fingers.

Soil: Cucumbers grow best in a well-drained sandy loam to clay loam soil
that is high in organic matter. A slightly raised well-drained bed may help
control certain diseases. The soil pH should be between 5.8 and 6.5.

Insects: The major pests that feed on cucumber are cucumber beetles, pickleworms, aphids, mites, whiteflies and the squash vine borer. **Solutions:** Spray with biologically friendly non-detergent soap mixed with water (1T per gallon water). Pick off and dispose of larger insects.

Diseases: Diseases that occur in the home garden include powdery and downy mildew, anthracnose, gummy stem blight, bacterial wilt, mosaic viruses, target spot and belly rot. Most of these diseases are not a problem in the spring except for bacterial wilt, which produces a powdery mildew in late spring. The others are mainly problems during the fall. **Solutions:** Use only high-quality seeds that have been treated with a fungicide. Avoid excessively wet soil and prolonged exposure to cool temperatures, conditions favorable to fungal disease.

Health Benefits: The silica in cucumbers is a major component contributing to healthy connective tissue, meaning muscles, tendons, ligaments, cartilage and bone. Cucumber juice is a good source of silica to improve the complexion and health of the skin, and the high water content makes it naturally hydrating, which is important for healthy-looking skin. Cucumbers are also used topically for various types of skin problems, including swelling under the eyes and sunburn. Two compounds in cucumbers, ascorbic acid and caffeic acid, prevent water retention, which may explain why cucumbers applied topically are often helpful for swollen eyes, burns and dermatitis.

Fulfilling your daily need for dietary fiber is not easy. Eating cucumbers, rich in fiber, helps. Add them to your salads for a quick and easy source of vitamins, fiber and fluids. In addition, you get the added benefits of silica, potassium and magnesium.

As if that weren't reason enough for eating cucumbers, they are beneficial in lowering high blood pressure.

Ready for the Kitchen: Cucumbers should be ready for harvest in about 50–70 days, depending on the variety. Pick as often as necessary to avoid oversized fruit, which can be pulpy and bitter. The more you pick, the more the vines will produce—one of the true joys of growing cucumbers. Harvest when cucumbers are about two inches long up to any size before they begin to turn yellow, in about 15 days. Remove fruit by turning cucumbers parallel to the vine and giving a quick snap. This prevents vine damage and results in a clean break. Store cucumbers in the refrigerator with the temperature between 45 and 50°F with a 95-percent relative humidity.

Annual Savings: Approximately $45 per year per person on average.

6

Lighting the Way

Within the pages of the hundreds — or perhaps even *thousands* — of indoor plant books, booklets and pamphlets in print today, you're going to run across countless false statements. I guarantee it.

Some of these statements will turn out to be relatively harmless. (One book I saw recently claimed that it is nearly impossible to start pine trees indoors from seeds; *au contraire!*) Other statements are outright ridiculous. (A very popular book I read claimed that plants should be given "good light but *never* direct sunlight." I still muse about just how plants have survived outdoors for millions of years under the "handicap" of full sun.) Still other gardening maxims can be downright harmful. (To kill off pests, spray lightly with a solution of vinegar and water... uh-huh.)

The point I'm trying to make is this: no matter how good the advice sounds, it must be tempered by your own experience and your individual growing conditions. In this book, I tell you of my experiences and those of other acknowledged experts in the horticultural field.

Fortunately, there are *some* universal truths about growing fruit and vegetables in pots. Among the most important is this: plants need light.

Lighting Up

A plant shop owner and "house call" specialist in Chicago once told me that up to three-quarters of the ailing plants he sees would be healthy if their owners realized how important *light* is to a plant's existence. He frequently finds people overestimating the amount of natural light available in certain areas or rooms. What they describe to him as "bright indirect light" often turns out to be very *low* light capable of sustaining few plants beyond the realm of the *Philodendrons* and a few varieties of ferns.

How does he know how much light is present in a room? He takes a photographic light meter into the homes he visits on his sick calls and measures every area of available light in foot-candle power. Most people are amazed to discover just how little light actually exists in a room they had thought to be "pretty bright."

What many people fail to realize is that what's bright to human beings is not necessarily bright to plants. Remember: many plants grow naturally in full, direct sunlight in their native environment. That's far more direct sunlight — especially in summer — than human beings could possibly endure for fourteen or sixteen hours a day. Think of what basking by the pool in direct summer sun would do to *you* in a few hours — let alone weeks or months! It's no wonder people have a tendency to overestimate the degree of brightness within their own homes.

Yet, unless you're a photographer used to taking light-meter readings and translating them to relatively easy-to-understand terms, the best you can hope for is a simple approximation of the level of brightness in your house. But with a few facts in mind, the process becomes less of a guessing game and more of an art.

Know Your Home's Exposures

It never fails to surprise me, when talking to fellow gardeners, how few actually know the various light exposures in their homes or what those different exposures mean for plants. Let me explain.

Most streets in most American neighborhoods (as well as many other places throughout the world) are arranged in grids running north and south, east and west. That means that most windows in our homes face in a specific direction and are said to have northern, southern, eastern or western exposures (as opposed to northeastern or southwestern exposures, etc.).

What exposures do your windows give you? Look straight out the window, off your balcony or beyond your patio toward the horizon. If you're looking south, that window is said to have a southern exposure. If you're looking east, it has an eastern exposure, and so forth.

Windows with a southern exposure receive the brightest light each day, all year long, and are thus said to have high-light exposures. Both eastern and western exposures receive light about half of the day and have medium or moderate light exposures (about half that of southern exposures), although western exposures receive their half-days of rays from the afternoon sun, which makes for stronger light than from the morning sun. A northern exposure receives the least amount of direct sunlight (if any) and is said to be a low-light exposure.

High-Light Heaven

I once knew a woman who lived in Wisconsin — hardly the banana belt of the universe. Despite that, she had a banana tree growing in her foyer. When she learned that I was a garden writer, she invited me over to see the clump of bananas the tree had borne on one of its stalks.

To say that I was amazed is an understatement. To say that I was green with envy would be closer to the truth. The fact is that, after viewing the 25-foot-tall specimen standing sentinel over the entranceway to her great room, I wanted one.

How, I wondered, could a tree that tall survive in a pot barely two feet in diameter — not only survive, but also bear exotic fruit!

After taking some light-meter readings, I got my answer. The spiraling sidewalls of clear glass and the sprawling skylights overhead provided the tree with only slightly less direct sunlight than it would have received growing wild in the Tropics. The whole-house humidifier that the woman had installed to help keep her asthma in check also provided the tree with the added humidity it needed to flourish.

I don't know if the woman ever got to harvest her crop of bananas in time. I moved away shortly thereafter. I do know, however, that, years later, I tried growing a banana tree of my very own in what I considered to be a brightly lighted foyer without an overhead skylight...and failed miserably.

All of which goes to show you: You can take a banana tree out of the Tropics and grow it in a container in Wisconsin, but you can't take the Tropics out of the container in Wisconsin and grow a banana tree just anywhere.

Or something like that.

Since different plants need different amounts of light, depending upon their natural growing conditions, you can position your plants throughout the house or outside to take advantage of the proper exposure for their maximum benefit.

Which spot in your home offers the greatest concentration of light? It's the southern exposure, as I explained. However, the light at that south-facing window is strongest nearest the pane. If you set a plant back from the glass only three feet, the light the plant's foliage receives is cut in half! That means that a plant set several feet away from a southern-exposure window is actually receiving much less light than full southern-exposure sun — perhaps the equivalent of a western or even an eastern exposure! If the plant requires the maximum light of a full southern exposure, the lack of light it receives from being set back so far from the window will eventually affect its growth and ultimately might even kill it.

Similarly, a plant that requires the moderate light of an eastern or western exposure isn't getting nearly enough light if it's set back three or four feet from an east- or west-facing pane. And pity the poor plant situated several feet back from a northern-exposure window. The light *that* plant receives is practically nonexistent! Only the most shade-loving plants can survive in an exposure such as that.

Scientists use a unit called the *foot-candle* to measure the amount of illumination from a given source. Technically, one foot-candle is equivalent to the amount of light cast on an object by one candle burning at a distance of one foot. Got that?

For a better idea of how wide a variance of light concentrations exists in a number of typical indoor situations, take a look at this lighting chart for everyday human *indoor* activities:

Homes

General illumination	5 foot-candles
Reading or writing	20 foot-candles
Ironing or sewing	40 foot-candles
Workbench	40 foot-candles

Hotels

Dining room	5–10 foot-candles
Lobby	20 foot-candles

Offices

Conference room	30 foot-candles
Typing area	50 foot-candles

Stores

Circulation areas	20 foot-candles
Merchandising areas	50 foot-candles
Display areas	100–200 foot-candles

Now, by comparison, take a look at the following chart, which shows the average amount of light available *outdoors* on various days.

Outdoors

Cloudy winter day	2,000 foot-candles
Sunny summer day	10,000 foot-candles

What these charts tell us is that, even on the cloudiest, dreariest, most wretchedly miserable winter's day, the light outside is *still* far greater than that available to plants indoors under average home lighting conditions.

So how does a plant suffer when it gets too little light? Does it get eyestrain? Become depressed? Turn surly? Die?

Actually, a plant shows no sign whatsoever of trouble from too little light — at first. Some plants can survive for fairly long periods of time off reserve food supplies in their roots. They don't require sunlight in order to manufacture enough food to sustain them through the process of photosynthesis. At least they don't for a while.

Think of it as an overweight person going on a 500-calorie-a-day starvation diet. One might expect him to lose at least five to ten pounds in three days, right?

Wrong. When a body receives little or no food for a short period of time, it converts small concentrations of stored fat into energy, and the body keeps right on going. It isn't until many days, weeks or even months later that the stored fat is eventually depleted, and the weight starts melting off.

It's a similar situation with plants. So long as a plant has a surplus supply of food, it will continue functioning normally. But if the plant receives so little light that it cannot manufacture sufficient food for itself to store, it will eventually become spindly and sparse. Its leaves will grow larger than normal in an attempt to allow the leaf surfaces to capture more light, and there will be fewer of them. The plant's stem will stretch hopelessly toward whatever little source of light exists. Finally, the lower leaves, and eventually *all* the leaves, will begin dying off.

In the case of flowering plants, the leaves may receive enough light to sustain adequate foliar (green) growth but not enough to produce flowers or set fruit. The entire process may take as long as a year or more, or it could transpire in a matter of weeks. Eventually, the light-starved plant will die.

The cure, of course, is to give the plant more light so that it can begin manufacturing food full-force once again. But be careful when making lighting corrections to plants that have been on restricted-light diets for some time. Never plunge a plant from one extreme into the other. A lettuce plant that has received minimal amounts of light for several months and is suddenly thrust into direct sunlight will suffer as much as or more so than if it had continued on its light-starvation diet. The key to increasing a plant's exposure to light is to give it more light *gradually*, so that it has time to adapt its system to the additional stimulus.

A few other factors besides exposure and nearness to a source of light also help determine how much light a plant receives. Dirt on a glass pane, for example, greatly reduces the amount of light entering a room. To give a plant all the available light possible, especially in northern exposures where light is at a premium, be sure to keep the glass clean inside and out.

Similarly, draperies, curtains, blinds and other window coverings reduce the amount of light entering a room, and you need to be aware of that before placing your plants near a covered window or sidelight.

Adding More Light

There are, lo and behold, several ways to increase the light in your home, even if you live in a cave. Thanks to good old American ingenuity (and the big houseplant boom that began several decades ago), numerous incandescent and fluorescent grow lights have flooded the market. For as little as three dollars, you can replace the bulb in a living room lamp with a special forty-watt or larger grow lamp to subsidize the natural light your plants receive. As a bonus, you'll get the spillover benefits — an

Inexpensive photographic studio lights such as this can be fitted with daylight-balanced bulbs and placed nearly anywhere to provide your plants with additional light. And they look good, too.

added boost of vitamin D, prevalent in natural sunlight and so necessary for human health and a strong immune system, as well.

If money is no object (and why would it be — we're all independently wealthy, aren't we?), you can set up an elaborate and mazelike system of ceiling track lighting. The system might feature several movable full-spectrum grow lamps that slide about the room and throw light exactly where you want it, when you want it.

I believe if I were reincarnated as a millionaire, I'd have a home designed with a series of light tracks stretching from one room to another, similar to a railroad switching yard, so that I could place my plants wherever I chose, even in the darkest, dingiest corner of my home. I would flick a switch, and the motorized grow lights would move around until they were ideally placed where I needed them most. Then I would simply sit back and watch things grow.

Of course, I'll wait patiently for that day. Until then, it's fortunate that there are so many more *affordable* grow-light systems available, some costing no more than a dollar or two above what a regular light bulb costs.

On one recent trip to my friendly discount department store, I bought a General Electric incandescent grow light for $3.95 and a porcelain-based reflector socket (recommended over plastic because of the high heat that grow lights often throw) for $5.95. The bulb was a 150 watter; yet, even with tax, the total was under $10.

Grow lights aren't the only answer to that dark-corner problem. If you have a spot begging for a plant, but there's no electrical outlet nearby and you don't want to invest in having an electrical outlet installed, you can benefit from a horticultural design trick I picked up years ago. Get two identical plants — say, high-light dwarf lime trees — and put one in the dark area, the other in a well-lighted southern exposure more suited to its growth requirements. After a week, change off. Continuing in that manner, you can keep both plants healthy and happy and producing fruit — at least to a degree — practically forever. And, of course, you'll accomplish your goal of filling that dark corner with exactly the plant you want.

In order to ease the pain of moving two large tubs, such as a couple of potted begonias, buy (or make) wooden trivets only slightly larger than the base of the pots and equip them with casters, which are available at hardware stores and home-improvement centers everywhere. If the plants' pots have bottom drainage holes, you can build water-tight drain pans into the trivets or set the pots in dishes. When "moving day" arrives, just roll the plants to their new locations. Any reasonably handy soul can slap a couple of trivets together in half an hour for only a couple of dollars.

On a Roll

Although it took some time to accomplish, I finally fitted movable trivets to the underside of every one of my large indoor pots. I used mark-free casters on the trivets so that I can roll them across tile, wood, carpeting or any other surface known to humankind without leaving any marks or doing any other damage. Of course, I didn't do that with my outdoor plants, because, well, they're out-of-doors.

That all changed a few months ago when I went to move a large outdoor pot planted with roses. The pot had been in the same location for a couple of years, and when I went to pull it out from behind the glider where it resided, it didn't budge. So I pulled harder…and harder, bending over at the waist and balancing precariously on one leg.

Finally, the pot broke free from its mooring, and I realized that its roots had grown through the pot's drainage hole and into the ground.

I thought no more about the incident until that evening, when I developed a twinge in my back. I was laid up, nearly totally incapacitated, for the next two weeks.

Now I have trivets on casters beneath all of my larger outdoor plants, too — a small enough price to pay for a healthy back!

Reflecting Light

Another way to multiply the effectiveness of existing light — whether natural or artificial — is to reflect it from where it exists to where it is that you want it. In a typical room, light passes through once, and whatever light the plants fail to catch is absorbed by walls, furniture, drapery and carpeting.

But if that unabsorbed light is reflected off the walls and back toward the containers, your plants will have a second chance at snaring those life-sustaining rays. In effect, the light entering the room will serve double duty.

The most effective way of reflecting light is the most expensive. For several hundred dollars or more, you can have someone come in and install full-length, wall-to-wall mirrors.

If you're resourceful, there's a viable option. Go to a hardware store or a home-supply center and pick up some mirror tiles to install yourself. With tiles, you can mirror exactly that portion of the wall you choose, at far less cost than having full-length mirrors professionally installed.

Or, less costly still (and far more creative), use wallpaper paste to hang sheets of foil-faced paper or even everyday aluminum foil (shiny side out). When working with foil, you'll have to be careful, since it tears easily.

After the foil is up, crisscross it with a lattice made of ordinary wood lath painted to complement or contrast with your wall colors. (White will reflect the most light.) Depending on how you install the lattice, the foil will appear as little squares or diamonds, which not only reflect light, but also lend an illusion of depth to the room. You will have created a marvelous reflecting wall while adding a design detail that could end up looking stunning!

If you're not up for all that pasting, sawing and hammering, there's yet another option — so long as you're willing to settle for smaller re-flecting areas. Go to an artists' supply shop or craft store and buy some stretcher strips to make a frame the size of your choice. (The strips sim-ply slide together to create frames in a wide variety of sizes, twelve by twelve inches, forty-eight by seventy-two inches or whatever size you desire.) At home, assemble the strips and then "stretch" them with alu-minum foil (the way an artist would stretch canvas on them). Fold the edges of the foil around the back of the frame and secure with staples, thumb tacks or tape. Then hang the frame as you would a painting. In fact, hang several of them in groupings for a decorative, as well as func-tional, touch.

As a viable alternative, you can purchase a framed mirror (often for only a few dollars on sale) and hang that in a position near the plant to reflect incoming light.

Of course, light is reflected from many other materials, as well, in-cluding painted walls. Remember, though, that the lighter in tone the color, the more reflective the wall. A pastel yellow or off-white wall will reflect far more light than a navy blue or black wall.

Also, semi-gloss and gloss paints reflect more light than do flat-finish paints. Many people make the mistake of attempting to brighten the cor-ner of a dark-blue room with some pretty perky flowering shrubs and plants. Often, repainting even a single wall in a lighter color is all the change necessary to both brighten up the room and help those plants survive.

Which is the best reflective surface available inexpensively? Believe it or not, a light-colored painted wall actually reflects more light than aluminum, according to tests conducted at the Rodale Experimental Farm in Emmaus, Pennsylvania. You can benefit from this fact by nailing lathing on to an artist's frame made from stretcher strips. Let your imagination go as you create a functional piece of white-on-white artwork to hang as a reflecting work of art. As with the aluminum foil "pictures," create several different sizes and shapes for an interesting and appealing grouping.

Don't Touch Those Walls!

I remember living at one time in a small apartment with a long list of leasing requirements, most of which began with "No..." Not the least of these rental restrictions was making holes in the walls. Back then, that meant not hanging mirrors, tiles, paintings or any other reflective materials on the walls for the benefit of my plants.

As an alternative, I constructed a free-standing screen composed of three separate panels joined by hinges. I finished the panels with white paint and a little drawing or something to break up the monotony and placed the screen next to my favorite high-light plant, a *Dracaena marginata*. The panels caught and reflected the light from a nearby window back onto the plant, and when I moved from the apartment two years later, both plant and landlord were reported doing well.

And I got my security deposit back.

In full!

Too Much of a Good Thing

How can you tell if your plants are receiving *too much* light? If you're watering the plants normally and the leaves begin to turn brown, get brittle and fall off, that's a sign of burn-out due to sun scald. Don't ignore the early symptoms. For some plants, too much light can be every bit as damaging as too little.

To remedy the situation, cut back on the amount of light showering the foliage by using window coverings, painting reflective surfaces with a darker color or moving the plant back from the source of natural light a foot or two — just the opposite of what you would do to give your plants more light.

Remember that light is an extremely important element in determining what plants you can grow effectively and where you can grow them. But it's not the *single* most important element to successful container gardening. That distinction, perhaps surprisingly, falls to an often-overlooked element we call water.

01:00   IN A MINUTE

- Plants need a sufficient amount of light to grow healthy and strong, and that's rarely as much as they receive.

- Be aware of the fact that southern exposures offer the greatest amount of light; western exposures the next greatest; eastern exposures the next greatest; and northern exposures — well, let's just say, good luck!

- You can add more light for your plants in a number of ways, both active and passive.

- Reflecting existing light onto your plants is a great way to boost the amount of light available to your plants quickly and easily.

Celery (*Apium graveolens*)

Habit: Upright

Cultivars: Numerous

Seed or Transplants: Seed

Pot Size: Small-to-Medium

Water: Water moderately, allowing soil to dry out between waterings. Too little water will turn leaves brown and brittle; too much will turn the leaves yellow. Adjust accordingly.

Comments: Growing celery requires a lot of light, six hours a day minimum, and a lot of water. If the light is morning and afternoon sun with a shady break around noon, so much the better. If the water is on a timer, better still. This makes celery a little more difficult to grow than most vegetables, but the results are worth the effort. For example, did you know that celery actually has *negative* calories? Being almost absent of calories, the process of eating this dieter's delight actually consumes calories, netting you a negative calorie meal or snack!

Seeds: Plant seeds to a depth approximately twice the thickness of the seed; water and tamp soil firmly. Cover pot with a clear plastic container

Celery (*Apium graveolens*)

or wrap, and wait for germination. Keep soil moist but not saturated, and keep pot out of direct sunlight to avoid overheating. Uncover at the first sign of sprouts. Thin to approximately one plant per ten inches for maximum growth.

Insects: Although celery is fairly insect-resistant, the leaf miner loves to attack the delicate soft leaves, causing cosmetic damage. Also susceptible to attacks from slugs, aphids and celery flies. **Solutions:** Spray for insects with biologically friendly non-detergent soap mixed with water (1T per gallon water).

Diseases: Leaf spot and blight are the most common problems. **Solutions:** Treat leaf spot with three tablespoons of cider vinegar (standard 5% acidity) mixed with one gallon water and spray in early morning on infested plants. For leaf spot and blight (and as a general fungicide), mix 1 tablespoon baking soda, 2½ tablespoons vegetable oil and one gallon of water. Shake thoroughly to form a suspension. Add ½ teaspoon of pure Castile soap, and spray on infected plants. Be sure to agitate the sprayer from time to time to keep mixture in suspension. Saturate both upper and lower leaf surfaces and spray some on the soil. Repeat every five to seven days as needed.

Health Benefits: Celery contains compounds called coumarins that help prevent free radicals from damaging cells, thereby decreasing the mutations that increase the potential for cells to become cancerous. Coumarins also enhance the activity of certain white blood cells, our bodies' immune-system defenders that target and destroy potentially harmful cells, including cancer cells. In addition, compounds in celery called acetylenics have been shown to stop the growth of tumor cells.

As a bonus, celery has been found beneficial in lowering cholesterol and high blood pressure while promoting cardiovascular health. And it's yummy dipped in peanut butter.

Ready for the Kitchen: When stalks are fully developed and a foot or so in height, usually about 110 days after planting. Cut off at base of plant and store in refrigerator crisper drawer. Discard the large outer stalks if too stringy, or use diced in soups; the inner stalks (the "heart") are best for eating raw.

Annual Savings: Approximately $13 per year per person on average.

7

Where To Grow

When you get right down to it, one of the biggest questions about container gardening is where. Where on earth are you going to grow your fruits and vegetables?

If you had a greenhouse or a solarium or a sprawling empty room with no purpose of its own and all kinds of natural light, the answer to that question might be obvious. *Well, where do you think?*

But few people have greenhouses or solariums or sprawling empty rooms, so the question of where to grow their plants is a very real one. In the living room? The basement? The attic? In the kitchen? The cellar? The guest room?

I could tell you that I don't have the answer to those questions, but I won't. The truth is that you can grow your container produce wherever you want. And, if you're at all like me, I'm betting you're not going to settle on a single location. Not in *this* lifetime.

As a matter of fact, I have containers full of fruits and vegetables everywhere around the house. But you'd never know it. That's because I have other plants — ornamental vines and shrubs and trees and more — in virtually every room.

That doesn't mean that I'm growing fruits and vegetables in every room in the house. I'm not. I'm growing them in the most hospitable places I have available for them. The other plants, in those "other" less hospitable places, are mostly decorative foliar plants — the *Ficus* trees and *Philodendron*, and *Dracaena* and *Aralia*.

In between, I have carefully and discreetly inserted various fruit and vegetable plants. Sometimes, in their own pots. Other times, as companion plants.

What it all boils down to, then, is where do you *want* to grow your fruits and vegetables in containers? Where will they look best, intrude upon your lifestyle the least and grow well? That might be a good place to start.

Now, I'm going to confess something here. I'm fortunate to have a sun room (sometimes called a solarium) in my home. Originally constructed as a deck off the rear of the house, someone somewhere along the home's checkered past had the foresight to enclose it with three walls and a roof so that now it's a cool place to hang out for the entire family, which consists of two adults, a couple of cats and a couple hundred assorted plants. The cats get priority, of course, with the plants not far behind.

Our sun room faces south with windows on all three sides. It is perfectly situated to take in the early morning eastern exposure, mid-day southern exposure and late-day western exposure. It also takes in all the high-light plants I can stuff into its approximately 200 square feet of floor space. (Let's not count the hanging plants for the moment.)

As you might guess, there is very little recreating that goes on in this room. We don't sit out there in the afternoon and drink tea. We don't have breakfast served to us there in the mornings. Truth be known, floor space is a bit hard to come by because of all the plants.

But that's really the purpose of having a sun room, isn't it? To utilize its sunny exposure to greatest advantage? Whereas that might once have meant sitting in a wicker chair and reading the current issue of *Town and Country*, things didn't quite turn out that way. If I want to read now, I head down to my office or the great room to do so. If I want to grow produce, I head for the sun room.

This is without a doubt the ideal place to grow plants. Some cacti, some succulents such as *aloe vera* and lots and lots of fruits and vegetables. The floor is ceramic tile, so if anything spills over onto it, there's no problem. The walls are mostly glass, so if anything splashes onto them, there's no problem. And the air — my God, the air in that room is so full of fresh oxygen you couldn't possibly believe how invigorating it is to walk in there; it's so sweet and pure that I wish the entire house were one giant sun room.

So, that's the very first place I would look to begin growing fruits and vegetables in pots. If you have a south-facing deck, you might want to explore the option of having it enclosed, the way mine was. You might find the cost negligible compared to the rewards of having a year-round growing room at your command.

If you don't have such a deck and need to make do without a sun room, don't despair. You probably have a south- or west-facing picture window, which means you have a great beginning for your container garden.

By now you're probably beginning to get the point. Despite what we said earlier about the ability to add light to any area in your home, the easiest and most logical place to establish a container garden is in a naturally well-lighted part of your home. Decide which windows have south- or west-facing exposures (the two highest light exposures available to you), and plan your attack from there.

How do you tell which direction is south? Well, you could ask your neighbor, but he might not know anymore than you do. Besides, you don't want to look like a navigational dropout.

An easier way to tell what's up and what's down on your imaginary compass is to observe where the sun rises in the morning and where it sets in the afternoon. The former is your eastern exposure; the latter is your western exposure. With the rising sun on your left and the setting sun on your right, the exposure directly in front of you is southern. The exposure in front of and to toward the left of you would be southeastern; the exposure in front of you and toward the right would be southwestern. Simple, no?

The fourth and last exposure, the one you don't ever want to discuss in mixed company, is your northern exposure (directly behind you when you're facing south), which is great for growing mold, mushrooms and frustrated. It's not all that spiffy for growing much of anything else.

Of course, you want to place your plants in the highest light areas of your home, as near to the windows (or glass doors, if you have them) as possible.

But remember that natural light is not the only light under which you can grow your plants. (See Chapter 6.) With the vast array of daylight-balanced bulbs and fixtures available today, you can place your plants near literally any window and supplement them with artificial light in order to have a successful container garden. I know one person who was so determined to grow plants in a window-less room that he actually built a potting bench inside a walk-in closet and grew his produce using supplemental light only. Now that's giving old Ma Nature a run for her money!

Regardless of the source of your plants' light, there are several things you can do to ensure a good crop of fruit and vegetables in most every room in your house. Here are a few of my favorite suggestions.

Kitchens: Often located at the very rear of the house so the cook will have easy access to the backyard garden (and the dog coming in the front door will have a clear shot at tracking up the entire house on his way to his water dish), most kitchens boast at least one door and win-

Here in the southwestern high-desert country, our dwarf lime and lemon trees do well in a northwestern exposure on the deck. In other areas of the country, they would probably fare better in a southern or even a southwestern exposure, depending upon the strength of the sun's rays.

dow. If the glass faces south, all the better. But regardless of the exposure, you can dramatically increase the light for plants in that window by replacing the existing glass with a new garden window (sometimes called a greenhouse window) — a mini-greenhouse that attaches to the outside of the house and allows access to the plants from inside. Prices start around $500 and go up from there, depending upon framing materials (wood, metal or vinyl), size and other variables. These windows extend outward from the house approximately 12–18 inches and give you two or three shelves on which to set plants. Consider the investment if you have a kitchen with an existing window.

If spending that kind of money on a home for your container plants is out of the question, look around for a small table that you can set in front of the window. In that way, you can typically place four or more planters before a single pane of glass.

As yet another option, you might buy or build a plant stand to place before the glass. Or attach a flower box to the *inside* of the window just below the sill and fill it with produce-bearing plants.

Living rooms: Most living rooms have large windows — often called picture windows — that let in a lot of light. Often people arrange their furniture in front of these windows, which always seems like a waste of good light to me (not to mention the fact that a strong southern or western exposure will fade your furniture's fabric faster than you can say "replacement cost").

Instead of stacking your furniture in front of the windows, consider arranging your container garden either on tables or — if the windows aren't too high off the floor — right on the carpet or hardwood flooring. Make sure to use a waterproof saucer beneath the planters to prevent excess moisture from contacting the floor. And always place a waterproof plastic membrane or a trivet beneath a water-permeable saucer (such as terra cotta) to prevent the moisture from seeping through the saucer and ruining your expensive carpeting. It's been known to happen.

Of course, picture windows are an excellent place to place your container garden, because the large amount of light they let in can compensate even for the stingiest of northern exposures.

As a design bonus, tall plants in the living room can add drama and elegance to nearly any décor; and small plants can be utilized as companion plants to larger ornamentals. Yucca trees with vining cucumbers, anyone?

Basements: These rooms rarely have a lot of natural light available to them, but they often have plenty of electrical outlets and lots of potential for doing extracurricular duty. Why not set aside an entire section of your basement for growing fruits and vegetables in containers? Lots of pots — or even one long custom-built planter — can supply plenty of fresh produce in the course of a single growing season. And you may not even need to be chic. Just how many people go down into your basement in the course of a growing season, anyway?

Attics: An often neglected and underutilized area where you store the Christmas decorations for 11½ months out of the year, your attic — if it can be ventilated in order to dissipate excess heat — could make a great growing room. Many attics already have windows in them, and all have access to electrical outlets. What better place to grow fruits and vegetables than in a naturally heated area of the house that is off the beaten path? Just remember that the high heat in many attics means you'll need to check the soil moisture of your plants often and water frequently, perhaps as often as daily.

Spare Rooms: These are particularly well suited to small groupings — rooms such as offices, studies, guest rooms and even exercise and media rooms. If you can picture a stately *Dracaena marginata* in a room, you should be able to envision the same room with a grouping of pepper plants and peas or even root crops.

Bathrooms: These are rooms you might not often associate with container gardens, but bathrooms can be nearly perfect for growing fruits and vegetables. Many modern bathrooms feature sunken tubs or Jacuzzis with lots of decking around them and natural light from a window or skylight overhead. Others have recessed lighting just made to hold daylight-balanced bulbs. What better place to set a grouping of vining plants such as cucumbers, miniature melons or squash, combined with a few decorative ferns and *coleus*? The high humidity naturally present in most bathrooms will help sustain the plants, and the space they need to spread out will bring you rewards every spring and fall.

Bedrooms: Far off the beaten path from guests, bedrooms make great places to grow any number of container plants. Most feature at least one window, and many have sliding or French doors to a veranda or deck outside. That makes these rooms a great place to grow fruits and vegetables in an otherwise often under-utilized space.

Does your bedroom have a single window? Consider a window shelf or a cabinet placed at window height to hold your container garden. Does it have a sliding glass door or French doors leading onto a balcony? If so, you're in container-plant Mecca. A grouping of plants placed inside the doors will probably get all the light they need to flourish without additional help, and another grouping outside on the patio or deck will similarly do well and be readily accessible for watering and harvests.

As a bonus, growing plants in the bedroom can actually make sleeping more healthful. Because plants take in carbon dioxide during the day and give off oxygen at night, you'll have the added advantage of snoozing comfortably in that Sealy Posturepedic while the plants next to your bed are generating life-sustaining oxygen to help keep you healthy. Who could ask for anything more?

There are other places in and round your home where you can grow plants, of course. Decks, patios, verandas, hallways — if you have a few feet of floor space, I can guarantee that some of that space is being under-utilized.

Why not correct the situation by placing a plant or two in just the right spot to satisfy their growing needs? You'll be putting that otherwise dead space to good use and providing for a continuing supply of fruits and vegetables to see you through the year.

01:00   IN A MINUTE

- Turn a deck or patio into an enclosed sun room for year-round container gardening.

- Add a window box or a garden window to your kitchen to provide extra growing space for your fruits and vegetables.

- Utilize the unused space in your home by strategically placing potted plants in various locations.

- Protect costly flooring from water damage by placing a waterproof pad or trivet beneath water-permeable saucers.

Dwarf Apple (*Malus*)

Habit: Tree

Cultivars: Apple trees on M.26 rootstock generally will grow 10–12 feet tall. M.26 is a cold-hardy rootstock. Occasionally, trees on M.26 rootstocks may tend to tip or lean, in which case you may need to stake the tree to keep it upright.

Seed or transplants: Grafted hybrids

Pot Size: Large to extra large

Water: Water container thoroughly, allowing the soil to dry out between waterings. Too much moisture can lead to fungal diseases.

Comments: True dwarf apple trees will be about 30 to 40 percent as large as a standard tree, or approximately 8–12 feet tall at maturity, and may require support by a trellis or post. The most common dwarf rootstocks are M.9 and M.26. Trees grown on M.9 are the smaller of the two.

Apple varieties must be cross-pollinated to set fruit. This means that apple flowers must have pollen from a different apple/crabapple variety in order to set fruit. This is why you must plant two different apple varieties (unless you have a wild crabapple nearby), which is a good reason to keep your potted apple tree outdoors throughout the growing season.

Seeds: N/A

Transplants: Place in hole no deeper than original root ball, and tamp around stem firmly with your fingers.

Soil: When fruit trees arrive from the nursery, open the bundles immediately. Soak the roots in water for 6 to 12 hours (especially if they are not moist) in order to reduce the likelihood of transplant shock. Before planting, cut off all broken or mutilated parts of roots with a sharp knife or pruning shears. Keep root pruning to a minimum. Create a hole in the potting mix large enough to receive the roots freely without cramping or bending from their natural position. Set the plant in place with the graft or bud union two inches above the soil line. Work soil in and around the roots. When the hole is half-filled, firm the soil lightly with your hands. Tamp firmly when the hole is filled. Do not place fertilizer in the planting hole or fertilize immediately after planting.

Dwarf Apple (*Malus*)

Most fruit trees, including apples, grow best when the soil pH is between 5.8 and 6.5.

Insects: Damaging insects are codling moth, mites, scales, aphids and fruit worms. **Solutions:** Spray with biologically friendly non-detergent soap mixed with water (1T per gallon water). Pick off and dispose of larger insects.

Diseases: Diseases common to apples are cedar apple rust, scab, black rot, bitter rot and fire blight. **Solutions:** Spray with appropriate natural fungicide. (See Chapter 15.) Avoid excessively wet soil and prolonged exposure to cool temperatures, conditions favorable to fungal disease.

Health Benefits: One a day, and who needs a doctor? It's really true. Apples have the unique ability to provide nutrients in a manner that distinguishes them from all other fruits and makes them *numero uno* in providing overall general health.

When it comes to a healthy heart, antioxidants are a major key. They protect our cardiovascular systems from oxygen-related damage. Apples contain a long list of phytonutrients working together as antioxidants. These include quercetin, catechin, phloridzin and chlorogenic acid. The skin contains most of the apple's important nutrients. Raw apples are higher in many nutrients and phytochemicals than are cooked apples. Unpeeled apples eaten raw are a terrific source of many potent phytochemicals, including ellagic acid and the flavonoids (especially quercetin). Fresh whole apples and fresh apple juice, for example, contain approximately 100–130 milligrams per 100 grams (roughly 3½ ounces) of chlorogenic, ellagic and caffeic acids. In cooked or commercially prepared apples, the content of these compounds drops to nearly zero.[13]

Apples are beneficial fruits, too, in that they provide approximately 15 percent of the daily value (DV) of fiber. This includes both insoluble fiber (i.e., cellulose) and soluble fiber (pectin). Studies have shown that both types of fiber can help keep your LDL cholesterol levels under control, and if you have LDL cholesterol levels that are too high, apples are your ticket back to good health. Studies have shown that as little as two ounces of apples per day (less than half a medium-sized apple) are effective cholesterol fighters. That means you need to consume only one medium-sized apple three days a week to reap the maximum benefits.

Apples have also been shown to reduce the incidence and severity of asthma attacks. In fact, apples have stood out among other fruits when it comes to general support of overall lung function and health. Flavonoids that are unique to apples (such as phloridzin) are believed to be responsible for supporting healthy lungs.

The bottom line: apples are as common as dirt, but they are not nearly so benign. Don't assume that, simply because they are everywhere, they are not so beneficial as the more exotic fruits. Apples present fiber, flavonoids and antioxidants in a way that is uniquely their own. So whether you eat them fresh off the tree, baked (with cinnamon and honey or stevia) or sliced in your salads, eat them. You'll reap the benefits.

Ready for the Kitchen: The tree may bear fruit in two to three years. When picking apples, it is important to be careful to avoid injuring the fruit. The apple should be removed from the spur by pulling upward and outward while rotating the fruit slightly. Apples should always be picked with their stems attached to the fruit; otherwise, they will not keep as long.

Annual Savings: Approximately $37 per year per person on average.

8

Wet n' Wild!

A friend of mine bought a stately dwarf lemon tree in a 14-inch pot. The plant stood more than four feet tall and boasted a head of lush, green foliage mottled with bright-yellow fruit. He was justifiably proud of his acquisition, and he gave his showplace plant a prominent spot near a southern exposure in the living room. It was his first experience with growing fruiting plants indoors.

Within two months, most of the lemons fell off the tree; several of the lower branches grew pale; and the leaves turned yellow. Finally, the plant began shedding the rest of its leaves. Before long, the entire plant looked like Charlie Brown's Christmas Tree. Something had gone wrong — *desperately* wrong.

Determined to save his proudest horticultural acquisition, he decided to take drastic action. His diagnosis: not enough water.

My friend boosted his watering regimen from once a week to every four days, then every three days. In between watering, he misted the plant daily. Nothing seemed to help.

Finally, he called me. He knew that I had a healthy lemon tree in my living room and thought I might be able to recommend a miracle cure.

Well, I knew at a glance what the trouble was. The leaf stems were puffy and swollen. The fallen growth was canary yellow. The soil was saturated. The roots below the surface were probably beginning to rot. The diagnosis: *overwateritis.*

Often, plants that have been over-watered aren't diagnosed until too late. By then, they're dead, drowned by the very life-sustaining element so necessary for their life. This particular lemon tree survived and is now growing as if nothing had ever been wrong. But in order to heal itself, the tree required five weeks of drought — not a single splash of water. Now, it receives a healthy watering about once a month, with smaller waterings weekly. That's a far cry from completely saturating the soil every three or four days!

My friend was one of many gardeners who believe that plants die only from too little water, never from too much. In fact, the opposite is true. More plants die from over-watering than from any other single thing their owners do wrong. Too much moisture in the soil prevents the tiny, hair-like fibrous roots from obtaining the oxygen they need to survive. As a result, the roots swell, weaken and begin to decay. Thus damaged, they're incapable of supplying the plant with the nutrients so necessary for life. In effect, first the plant drowns, and then it starves. Talk about a double whammy!

While it's true that many small houseplants, especially large plants in small three- or four-inch clay pots, need frequent watering, most people don't realize just how much water a *large* pot filled with soil can hold — or for how long. On top of that, plastic or glazed ceramic pots — the types so many container plants are grown in these days — slow down the process of evaporation far more than clay pots or wooden planters.

So how often *should* a container plant be watered?

Unfortunately, there is no watering timetable for *any* container plant. The only sensible and effective way of determining when a plant needs water is by using the two-knuckle test.

Drill your finger into the soil at least down to the second knuckle (about two inches) — deeper in larger pots. If the soil feels relatively dry on your fingertip, and if your finger comes out with little or no soil clinging to it, it's time for watering. If the soil feels moist, or if your finger comes out with a coating of soil, wait a day or two before testing again.

Of course, you have to temper your test with common sense. You need to dig deeper into a larger pot than into a smaller one to determine the soil's water content farther from the surface. Remember that the soil in a pot dries out first at the top, then gradually toward the bottom, where the plant's roots are most likely to be concentrated. If the soil on top feels dry to the touch, that doesn't mean it isn't saturated a couple of inches below the surface. Remember to dig that finger into the soil at least to your second knuckle. It's what's *below* the surface that counts.

Too Much or Not Enough?

If you discover your favorite plant turning funny shades of every color but green, the question is often, Am I over-watering or under-watering?

Generally speaking, if the leaves turn from lush green to dry, crackly brown, the plant isn't receiving enough water. Probably you're not thoroughly saturating the soil when you water, only wetting the surface. Make sure that the water runs from the drain holes in the pot before assuming that the plant is watered thoroughly.

However, if the leaves go from green directly to yellow and then fall off, you've fallen victim to *overwateritis*. In that case, cut back on your watering schedule immediately. If the plant shows little sign of improving within a week, it may need a pruning job (both leaves and roots) and repotting in fresh, dry soil. All you can do then is wait, adopt a more reasonable watering schedule and hope for the best.

After a few weeks of experience with touch-testing, most indoor gardeners get the hang of it. As with so many things in life, experience in this area is the best — in fact, the *only* — teacher. For those with weak fingers or an aversion to dirt, several manufacturers sell moisture meters consisting of a metallic probe that you stick into the earth and a gauge or dial for reading the results. When the gauge reads "dry," you water.

For me, that degree of mechanization takes a lot of the fun out of container gardening. I don't own any such gadgets, and I doubt that I ever will. If you really want to try one out, invest in a good one, one that will give you consistently accurate results. You'll find them available from many gardening centers and plant specialty shops or on the Internet.

Of course, the rule that you should allow your fruit and vegetable plants — or any plants, for that matter — to dry out between watering is only a generalization. Some plants require continuously moist soil, although they're certainly in the minority. Cranberry bushes, for example, prefer highly acidic, generally moist soil. Other plants that prefer to remain on the damp side between waterings are discussed in later chapters.

How Much Is Enough?

There's no magic formula by which you may deduce how *much* water is needed for a particular species of potted plant. But there *is* a not-so-magic rule of thumb that says: water *thoroughly*. Notice thoroughly, not *regularly.* If you give your tomato plants a few ounces of water every other day, you actually run the risk of killing them. While you may be moistening the surface and encouraging surface-root growth, you're neglecting the deep-down soil and discouraging deep-root growth. The first time the surface soil containing all the roots dries out, those roots concentrated near the top will dry out, too, and die. It's important to encourage deep-root growth through the practice of thorough watering.

How does one tell when the soil is saturated, especially in a deep pot where you can't prod more than a couple of inches into the soil? There's only one sure way. You know you've watered enough when the excess water runs out of the pot's drainage hole. The amount of water required will depend on the location of the plant in the home (plants dry out more quickly, remember, in the heat of direct sunlight than in much cooler partial shade) as well as the growth pattern of the plant, the composition of the soil, the time of year and even the material from which the pot is made.

In watering a plant with no drainage holes in the pot (a potentially dangerous situation that calls for more than a little experience and wise judgment on the part of the gardener), use a little trick horticulturists use. First, stuff the neck of a funnel into the soil. Then measure a quart of water into a jar. Fill the funnel to the top, and watch how much of the

(*left*) This plant shows signs of not receiving enough water. Note the brown leaf edges, which will slowly work their way toward the leaf stem. In time, the entire plant will wither and die. (*right*) This plant shows signs of receiving too much water. The yellow tips on the leaves are the first sign of over-watering, a warning that the delicate fibrous roots are beginning to rot and die off.

liquid seeps into the pot. If all of it disappears within a relatively short period of time, measure out some more. When no more water seeps out of the funnel, the soil is saturated — that is, it's been watered thoroughly and will not hold any more moisture.

At that point, put your finger into the funnel and against the hole to prevent the remaining water in the funnel from leaking out all over the floor. Extract the funnel and pour the excess water back into the jar. Check to see how much of that initial quart (or half gallon, etc.) the plant actually took. If it took six ounces of water to saturate the pot, you'll know you should give the plant no more than six ounces (or a little less, to be on the safe side) the next time it needs watering. As a result, you won't have to go through the time and trouble of fussing with a funnel at every watering.

Still Waters Run Deep

I once made the brilliant discovery that any pot — even the ugliest pot on earth — can be dressed up by placing it inside a decorative container. Ecstatic, I purchased several decorative wicker baskets and set saucers in the bottom before placing the potted plants inside the saucers.

A few weeks later, I was disheartened to see that the plants were beginning to yellow and drop their leaves. Knowing that the soil was good, the light was right and I wasn't over watering (I used the finger test), I decided to treat the plants with a nitrogen-based fertilizer. The plants perked up for a few days before sinking to a new low.

Finally, I lifted the pots out of their decorative wicker containers and found the culprit — water sitting in the saucers. While the tops of the pots were dry to the touch, the bottoms — where most of the plants' roots congregate — were saturated.

I emptied the saucers of the standing water, filled them with medium-sized pebbles and set the pots back inside the wicker containers. Then I withheld water for a week to give the soil a chance to dry out again. Now, if I do over water, the excess water runs down past the pebbles into the saucers, but the pots — resting on top of the pebbles — remain above the standing water.

A Rose by Any Other Name

When it comes to the source of the water you use for watering your plants, once again, you'll need to experiment. Some people make a point of using only bottled or distilled water, claiming that tap water contains too much chlorine and other harsh chemical additives.

In reality, tap water is usually fine. If you live in an area where the water is heavily chlorinated, though, allow it to stand in an open jar or watering can overnight to help neutralize the chlorine.

Also, I've heard over the years that soft water — the kind that's treated by a home water softener before flowing through your taps — is bad for plants. It supposedly adds sodium (salt) to the water, which can be toxic to most plants. I've never had anything die because of soft water — not that I can recall, in any event. But, if you'd prefer not to take a chance, draw your plants' water from the outside spigot (such water is nearly always left untreated for economy's sake). Bring the water inside and let it warm to room temperature before using it on your plants. In fact, you should *never* use cold water for any of your houseplants. Water that is too cold can actually shock a plant, sometimes beyond recovery.

Humidity

Another aspect of healthy plant growth is the amount of humidity present in the plant's environment: it's rarely enough. In winter, especially in drier western or northern climates, there's hardly enough humidity to suit *our* needs, as our own dry, flaking skin will attest. Too much dry air can lead to dry, aching throats and swollen, blocked sinus passages. Most plants respond to dry air similarly poorly.

Without sufficient moisture, a plant's leaves will lose their brilliant leathery look and deep green coloration. Their tips and edges may turn brownish yellow; minor cuts and scrapes may fail to heal properly, if at all.

On very cold nights in the Midwest, I've seen the hygrometer dip to as low as 25 percent. In the Southwest, it's even lower. That kind of relative humidity is extremely uncomfortable to humans and potentially dangerous to plants. When you remember that some plants — especially those native to the Tropics — enjoy as much as 75 or 80 percent humidity in their native environment, it's not hard to understand just how badly humidity is needed.

The big question is, of course, *how* to add it.

When dealing with small potted plants, you can follow the instructions in those wonderful little books that tell all about filling a tray with pebbles, setting the plants in the tray and keeping the pebbles half covered with water. The evaporating water provides a moist mini-environment surrounding the plants. Or so they say.

The only problem with that solution is that the dampened tray system doesn't work for other than the smallest of pots. Nearly as quickly as the water vaporizes and rises from the tray, it is absorbed by the warm, dry air surrounding it and dissipated before it ever reaches the plant's leaves where it is needed most.

Besides, when growing fruit and vegetables in pots, most trays filled with pebbles and water will be large and awkward to handle. Try keeping a hundred-pound potted fig tree humidified by pouring water over a tray full of pebbles!

Instead of the pebbles-in-the-tray trick, the most efficient, albeit expensive, way of beating the dry-air blues is to add an automatic humidifier to your home's forced-air heating system. You can set the humidistat to the degree of humidity you want, and the device does the rest. After all, for between a few hundred and a few thousand dollars, it ought to work out just peachy.

Other humidifiers work just as well on a smaller scale. Many manufacturers make single-room models holding up to seven or eight gallons of water. When the humidity level in the surrounding area drops to a certain point, the machine clicks into action, sending moisture pulsing into the air. Prices for portable humidifiers are considerably lower than those for whole-house models, of course, and most such units are equipped with wheels so that they can be moved easily from one area to another.

Somewhat less efficient and holding less water are devices typically used for treating respiratory problems. These units hold a gallon or two of water and safely spit it out in the form of either cool mist or warm steam, depending on the model. Not the best solution to the problem, but certainly better than nothing.

If you're opposed to spending money for *any* type of humidification system, don't give up hope. You can still add humidity to your indoor trees on a plant-by-plant basis.

Taking a tip from the pebble-and-tray people, you can spread a layer of peat moss *on top of the potting mixture* and keep the moss damp by misting it daily. When you touch-test the soil for the purpose of deciding when to water, just remember to move the moss aside and dig your finger down into the potting mix, not merely into the wet moss, to tell whether or not it's time to water.

Another way to add humidity to your plants is to spray them daily — more often, if you have the time and inclination. The spray will settle on the plant's leaves, as well as on the soil, and add moisture to the air immediately around the plant, helping to keep the plant's leaves cool, refreshed and healthy as it vaporizes.

The drawback to this system is that, as soon as the small droplets of moisture evaporate, the plant is thrust back into the dry climate of its surroundings, meaning you have to be vigilant in misting again to have any appreciable effect on the humidity available to the plant.

If you're looking for a way to mist your outdoor containers, here's an idea I hit upon several years ago. Go to your local hardware store or home improvement center and buy a relatively inexpensive misting system designed to cool the ambient outdoor air by as much as 10–20 degrees. They are designed to keep people more comfortable in the dog days of summer, but they work wonderfully well for plants, too. In fact, my plants thrive beneath them.

The system attaches to a hose bib and, by turning the outdoor spigot on and off, you can really do the trick. For more controlled results, place a timer between the bib and the misters and set the timer for a prescribed number of minutes each day — or even several times a day, as required.

Be careful not to mist your plants too much, as these systems can put out a tremendous amount of humidity that condenses into water in just a few minutes' time.

How Hot Is Hot?

Once you have the light, water and humidity aspects of container gardening down pat, the question comes up: How hot is hot? Contrary to popular horticultural belief, hotter isn't necessarily better. In fact, for most plants, heat without a correspondingly high level of humidity can be very damaging. The average home — even one equipped with a central humidifier — simply can't provide sufficient moisture to prevent plants from drying out at 78–80°F, *period*. The hot air near radiators, vents or other sources of heat dries out plants even more rapidly, so you should avoid keeping plants next to such heat sources whenever possible.

Ideally (for the plants, that is), the indoor temperature should be held to 66–68°F during winter, because it's relatively easy to humidify dry winter air at that temperature, more difficult as the temperature rises. For every additional degree, an increasingly larger volume of moisture is required to raise the humidity one point.

But beware! In your efforts to keep your home cool, don't fall prey to the trap at the other end of the spectrum. Cool is good; cold *drafts* are not. Be sure to keep all plants away from leaky windows and outside doors during the winter months and from powerful fans and air-conditioner outlets in the summer. While moving air provides good circulation and is actually healthy for plants, the air should be no cooler or warmer than a degree or two outside of the ambient room temperature.

How Are Things in Casablanca?

It's a cute subtitle, I know. But aside from that, it has a point. Indoor plants actually grow very well in Casablanca, thank you very much, for several reasons. First, the heat (it's hot!). Second, the humidity (it's high!). Third, those adorable ceiling fans that were (and are once again) the rage. Ceiling fans do more than look nice — especially for indoor plants. They keep the air *moving*. That's very important for healthy plants. By continuously providing container plants with moving air, fans can prevent plant leaf surfaces from overheating. Moving air also helps to discourage the formation of fungus and mold on damp soil and in the axels of plants' leaf stems.

If your home isn't equipped with a ceiling fan, you can create the same effect by placing a small portable fan so that air blows against a blank wall and then bounces back into the room, gently swishing your plants' leaves.

A simpler way of aerating a room, so long as you don't live in the Sahara, is to open the windows. Gentle summer breezes can do wonders for a plant's general health. Sometimes twentieth-century people, in all our wisdom, tend to forget just how wise in her simplicity Mother Nature can be.

01:00   IN A MINUTE

- Over-watering plants is the single greatest mistake most amateur gardeners make.

- To know when your plants require water, use a high-tech moisture probe or the considerably lower-tech "finger-in-the-soil" method, both equally effective.

- Humidity is beneficial for most potted plants, both indoors and out.

- Keep your potted plants away from heating and cooling sources and out of the direct stream of house fans to prevent them from drying out.

Beets (*Beta vulgaris*)

Habit: Root

Cultivars: There are numerous cultivars available, but three in particular for easy growth and good production are:
  - Detroit Dark Red, Red Ace and Red Cloud

Seed or Transplants: Both

Pot Size: Medium

Water: Water moderately, allowing soil to dry out between waterings. Too little water will turn leaves brown and brittle and retard the production of the root; too much will turn the leaves yellow and stunt the root. Adjust accordingly.

Comments: Beets require full sun and uniform fertilizing and watering during their growth cycle. However, beets can be harvested at any stage in their development, including the sprouts (usually eaten raw or tossed in salads) during the thinning out stage. They are high in beneficial vitamins and minerals.

Seeds: Plant seeds to a depth approximately twice the thickness of the seed; water and tamp soil firmly with your fingers. Cover pot with a clear plastic container or wrap, and wait for germination. Keep soil moist but not saturated, and keep pot out of direct sunlight to avoid overheating. Uncover at the first sign of sprouts. Thin to approximately one plant per six inches. Retain thinnings for use as sprouts in soups, salads and other dishes.

Beets (*Beta vulgaris*)

Transplants: Place in hole no deeper than original root ball and tamp around stem firmly.

Soil: Beets prefer soil that is loamy or sandy. Hard clay soils prevent root enlargement. Beets require full sun and will not make good roots in partial shade. Protect beet seedlings from the wind because the young plants can dry out rapidly.

Insects: The most common insect pests of beets are aphids, leaf miners, flea beetles and webworms. **Solutions:** Spray for insects with biologically friendly non-detergent soap mixed with water (1T per gallon water).

Diseases: Cercospora leaf spot is the most common disease that occurs on beets. Circular spots with reddish brown or purplish margins are the first signs. Beets are also very susceptible to damping-off and root-knot nematodes. Beets will develop internal black spot if soil boron is not adequate. **Solutions:** Use boron at planting according to directions.

Health Benefits: The next time you ask yourself why you should eat beets, remember all of those legendary Russian centenarians. Beets, frequently consumed either pickled or in borscht, the traditional Russian soup, may be one reason behind their longevity and health. These ruby-red root vegetables contain powerful nutrients that help to protect against heart disease, birth defects and certain cancers, particularly cancer of the colon. Betacyanin, the pigment that gives beets their rich crimson color, is also a powerful cancer-fighting agent.

As a bonus, the beet's leaves are edible either steamed or raw and contain even more nutrients than the bulb.

Ready for the Kitchen: May be harvested at any stage, although ideally the bulbs should not be allowed to grow larger than 2–3 inches in diameter, or they are likely to be fibrous and tough. Full maturation is typically 50–60 days from seed. Save the leaves for salad tossings.

Annual Savings: Approximately $24 per year per person on average.

D.J. Herda

Celery
Celery is healthful and easy to grow in most environments. It can also be allowed to go to seed, which can be used in cooking or dried and ground for future use.

Lettuce
All lettuce is easy to grow, although leaf lettuce grows like a weed! Harvest the largest leaves first, and the plant will continue producing for several more weeks before getting "woody."

D.J. Herda

Companion Planting
Mixing marigolds with nearly any fruits and vegetables is a great way to discourage aphids and other pests from attacking — and a good way to dress up a container!

Kitchen Produce
All of these crops were harvested from containers — some inside and the others outside on our decks and patios.

Figs

Figs are easy to grow and high in vitamins and minerals. They also dry well for use all winter long.

Fig Tree

Figs are ready for harvest when they break free of the branches with very little encouragement. The leaves from the fig tree can also be used as a healthful wrap when steaming fresh fruits or vegetables.

Citrus Trees

When the weather turns cold, you'll need to protect delicate plants. We move ours, including our dwarf citrus trees, into a cool storage room near a northern-exposure window. Outside of a few fallen leaves, the trees do just fine.

D.J. Herda

Marinara Sauce
We enjoy preparing our vegetables and herbs for homemade marinara sauce right from the containers in our own sunroom.

Herbs
An easy way to add herbs to your sauce: pick them, bunch them, and tie them together with cooking string before dropping the bouquet into the sauce. Simmer on low for at least 30 minutes.

Nasturtium

We utilize every place imaginable for our container gardening — including cedar window boxes attached to the fence. This one holding two varieties of edible Nasturtiums offers us a colorful and healthy addition to our summer salads.

Thyme

The south-facing window box outside my office is a great place to grow herbs, such as oregano and this fragrant thyme.

D.J. Herda

D.J. Herda

Hot Peppers

Hot peppers are among the easiest of plants to grow. Surprisingly, horn worms will attack the fruits, so pick and squash the insects as you find them.

D.J. Herda

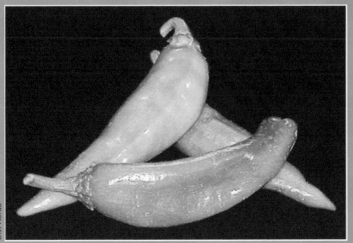

D.J. Herda

Anaheim Peppers

Anaheim peppers add a tasty zest to a meal without being overwhelmingly hot. They're also delicious (and very healthful!) served raw in fresh salads.

Watercress

The plants in the center of one of our ponds are watercress. They grow all year long and spread like crazy. We purchased a sprig with roots still attached from the grocery store, planted it in a pot filled with pea gravel, and placed the container six inches below water level. We harvest the leaves for salads every few days.

D.J. Herda

9

The Right Stuff

Dirt is dirt is dirt. Isn't it?

Well, yes, I suppose it is. Unfortunately, we don't grow container plants in dirt or garden soil or anything else that is naturally occurring. At least not without a few modifications.

But, you ask, if dirt is good enough for growing fruits and vegetables outdoors in the ground, why not indoors in pots?

The answer is simple: contaminants.

I'm not talking about radioactive strontium 90 or toxic lead or mercury or even DDT. (Let's hope none of those elements are present in your garden soil.) I'm talking about things such as disease organisms and insects.

Let's face it. Lots of things reside in everyday garden soil — both beneficial and not so beneficial. The fact that plants can grow and survive in and actually prosper from such soil is a wonder in itself. But outdoor plants have their own natural cleansing mechanisms. Roots that find themselves growing in contaminated soil can reach out to other areas of the garden. Harmful insects that sprout from eggs in the ground may soon fall victim, themselves, to predatory insects such as ladybugs and preying mantises, which thrive in the garden. Even fungus that threatens to consume a plant can be affected by the drying effects of sun and wind.

Plants growing in a container filled with contaminated garden soil, though, aren't so fortunate. When *they* get attacked, they have little hope for survival but you.

Sure, you can turn to the appropriate insecticide, fungicide and bactericide, but why bother? Why not make sure the soil is safe for indoor use in the first place and skip all that extra trouble? Who needs the hassles?

No, garden soil is called garden soil for a reason. Leave it where it is. Or, if you're determined to avail yourself of the soil right outside your door, at least plan on sterilizing it. To do that, you'll need to place the soil in a suitable container, such as a metal bowl or a roasting pan, and pop the mixture into an oven preheated to 180°F. Allow it to bake for 30–45 minutes. Halfway through, turn the soil with a garden trowel to make sure it heats evenly.

After the soil has been sterilized and cooled, amend it by adding pine bark (for nutrition and moisture retention), peat moss (for water retention), Perlite (for loosening heavy soil) or sand (to improve the physical structure) as required.

But be forewarned. When you heat garden soil in the oven, you're going to notice a unique odor that many people find objectionable. That's because you're killing off living organisms and releasing the aromas from various organic compounds into the air.

Analyzing Your Garden Soil

If you do decide to use your own sterilized garden soil, you may need to amend it for consistency so that it is suitable for what you'll be growing. To tell what's in your soil, you can either take a sample to your local horticultural agent and have him test it scientifically, or run your own test. The latter is somewhat cruder and less detailed but relatively reliable.

To test your soil yourself, start by sprinkling your garden soil lightly and waiting a couple of hours. Dig up a handful of the soil and squeeze it tightly inside one fist. Open that fist and examine the soil.

If it crumbles apart on its own, it needs organic matter (pine bark, mulched tree leaves, peat moss, etc.) to give it more body. If it doesn't crumble even when you prod it, it has too much clay in it and needs more coarse sand and Perlite. If it crumbles lightly only *after* you prod it, the consistency is probably just right.

This test won't tell you what nutrients the soil has, of course, but it will give you a good idea of the approximate content of the soil, or the soil type. Soil that is too crumbly is probably lacking in nutrients and will not hold moisture well. Soil that is too tight similarly lacks nutri-

(*left*) Using a garden trowel, dig up a handful of soil and cup it in your palm. (*right*) Squeeze the soil tightly for several seconds before opening your palm. Check the soil for consistency, making whatever adjustments are necessary based upon your evaluation.

ents, holds too much moisture, does not allow for oxygen penetration and may block healthy root growth.

Soil that is just right is the best of all worlds — "bitey" enough to hold the plant upright, yet friable or light enough to allow moisture and oxygen to penetrate to the roots.

You can also test your soil for alkalinity — the degree to which the soil is either alkaline or acidic. Various home-use testing kits are available with instructions on how to increase or decrease your soil's pH level.

Using a Commercial Mix

If the thought of squeezing garden soil in your fist and smelling the seductive aroma of freshly roasted dirt in the house for several hours fails to appeal to you — or if you simply don't want to go through all the hassle — here's the good news: You don't have to. You can buy or make a high-quality container mix that:

- is dense enough to support the plants,
- has sufficient nutrient-holding capacity,
- allows water and air to pass readily through the mix while retaining adequate moisture and
- is free of insects, diseases and weed seeds.

Most commercially prepared potting-soil mixes are not actually soil at all but rather a combination of organic matter, such as peat moss or ground pine bark, and inorganic material, such as washed coarse sand,

Perlite or vermiculite. Vermiculite loses its structure relatively quickly, though, and should be used only for propagating young plants or seedlings as opposed to long-term gardening.

Many indoor gardeners use a potting mixture that contains a combination of peat moss and Perlite, with enough sand and pine bark thrown in to give the mixture body. The result is a soil-free, sterile and lightweight mix in which most potted plants thrive. High-quality commercial mixes also often contain slow-release fertilizers that supply the plant's needs for at least a few months. These nutrients are usually low in trace or minor elements, though, so you'll still need to supplement your plants periodically.

Commercially prepared mixes vary in price, ingredients and physical and chemical characteristics, so you'll have to try a few different brands before deciding which one works best for you. Buy a few small bags of several different potting mixes and spend a week or two deciding which you like best.

And remember that potting soil (potting, as in the word, "pot") is not the same as garden soil or planting mix. Make sure the bag you buy says *sterilized* potting soil for indoor use and not unsterilized soil for general outdoor use.

You also can prepare your own artificial potting medium simply by following one of these suggested recipes:

1. Two parts peat, one part Perlite, one part coarse sand (also called contractor's sand, available at most home centers and nurseries)
2. Two parts peat, one part coarse sand
3. One part peat, one part coarse sand, one part pine bark
4. One part peat, one part pine bark, one part Perlite

Once you have the basic potting mix prepared for planting, don't forget that you'll also have to feed your plants throughout the growing season. Fruits and vegetables are heavy feeders. They require a good supply of all the proper nutrients not only to generate strong, healthy foliar growth but also to produce and set flowers and bear fruit. We'll talk more about the types and amounts of nutrients you should feed your plants later.

Remember that the purpose of soil is multi-fold. It provides protection for the plant's delicate roots; it holds necessary moisture and nutrients for release as the plant requires them; and it prevents the plant from falling over.

It's important to have the right combination of elements in your potting soil to accomplish all of these goals effectively.

01:00   IN A MINUTE

- Never use soil straight from the garden for your container plants.

- If you want to use garden soil, sterilize it first in a 180°F oven for 30–45 minutes to kill off contaminants.

- You can make your own soil-free potting mix by using varying quantities of peat moss, Perlite, Vermiculite, pine bark and coarse sand.

Eggplant (*Solanum melongena*)

Habit: Bush

Cultivars: Some of the best for container gardening include:

- *Regular types:* Black Magic (hybrid), Purple Rain (hybrid), Early Bird (hybrid) and Little Prince (compact hybrid)
- *Long types:* Ichiban (hybrid) and Pintung Long

Seed or Transplants: Both

Pot Size: Medium

Water: Water to a depth of at least six inches. Morning watering is best so that the leaves dry out before evening, discouraging various fungal diseases.

Comments: The standard eggplant produces egg-shaped, glossy, purple-black fruit six to nine inches long. The long, slender Japanese eggplant has a thinner skin and more delicate flavor. White ornamental varieties are edible but have poor eating quality. Eggplant is a warm-season vegetable that grows best when temperatures are between 70–85°F. It enjoys a long growing season, provided it is not exposed to frost. Start seed indoors eight to nine weeks prior to the outdoor planting date. Seeds germinate quickly at 70–90°F.

Seeds: Plant seeds to a depth approximately twice the thickness of the seed; water and tamp soil firmly. Cover pot with a clear plastic container or wrap, and wait for germination. Keep soil moist but not saturated, and keep pot out of direct sunlight to avoid overheating. Do not expose to cold. Uncover at the first sign of sprouts. When three sets of leaf axils form, thin to approximately one plant per six inches.

Transplants: Purchase eggplant transplants from a reputable garden center to ensure that the plants are the best quality. Do not purchase tall, spindly plants or plants that have blossoms. (Blossoms on the transplants will slow their growth after transplanting and may result in a lower yield.) Place plantlets into a hole no deeper than original root ball, and tamp around stem firmly with your fingers.

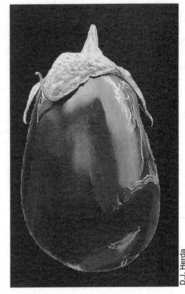

Eggplant (*Solanum melongena*)

Soil: Eggplant grows best in a well-drained sandy loam or loamy soil, fairly high in organic matter. The soil pH should be between 5.8 and 6.5 for best growth and fruit production.

Insects: Watch for Colorado potato beetles, flea beetles, lace bugs, tomato hornworms and mites. Damage often consists of small, bullet-wound type holes in the leaves. Keep outdoor potted plants covered beneath clear plastic until they are large enough to tolerate leaf damage. **Solutions:** Spray for insects with biologically friendly non-detergent soap mixed with water (1T per gallon water).

Diseases: Commonly seen diseases in eggplant include Phytophthora blight, bacterial wilt and Phomopsis blight. **Solutions:** Choose resistant varieties and keep misting and moisture in general to a minimum. For infected plants, try baking soda spray fungicide. (See Chapter 15.)

Health Benefits: In addition to offering a wide range of vitamins and minerals, eggplant contains crucial phytonutrients, many of which have antioxidant properties. These phytonutrients include the phenolic compounds (phenols), such as caffeic and chlorogenic acid, and the flavonoids, including nasunin.

The skin of eggplant is also beneficial, according to the findings of numerous studies. Nasunin in the eggplant's skin is a potent antioxidant and a free radical scavenger that has been shown to protect cell membranes from damage. In animal studies, researchers found that nasunin protects the lipids (fats) in brain cell membranes. These lipids are responsible for protecting the cells from free radical damage, allowing nutrients in and ushering waste matter out.

Ready for the Kitchen: May be harvested as soon as fruit appears swollen and fully colored, about 10 inches in length or more, usually in about 70 days from seed.

Annual Savings: Approximately $32 per year per person on average.

From Alkaline to Acidic: The Magic of pH

Americans spent roughly $50 billion on their lawns and gardens in 2008 in an effort to keep them looking good and producing healthy fruits and vegetables. Unfortunately, it's a good bet that much of that money was wasted.

Why? The answer can be summed up in one word: pH.

What, you ask, is pH? It's a means of measuring the alkalinity or acidity of something. The pH of your soil or potting mix is important to know because the degree of alkalinity/acidity directly affects the availability of nutrients to your plants. Too much of either, and your plants will find the nutrients you give them "locked up" and unavailable for use. And nutrients, as you know, are critical to a plant's growth.

Measurements of pH are made along a numerical scale ranging from 0–14, with 7 being "neutral." Numbers on the scale below 7 indicate an acidic soil, while numbers above 7 indicate alkalinity.

The pH value of soil is one of a number of environmental conditions that affect the quality of plant growth. Different plants thrive best in different soil pH ranges. Azaleas, rhododendrons, blueberries and conifers, for example, thrive best in acidic soils (pH 5.0–5.5). Vegetables, grasses and most ornamentals do best in only mildly acidic soils (pH 5.8–6.5). Chicory and Russian olive do best in slightly alkaline soils (pH 6.5–7.2).

Soil pH values outside of these ranges will very likely result in nutrient deficiencies in your plants. And nutrient deficiencies mean smaller yields and smaller produce.

Obviously, it makes sense to grow plants in a soil with a pH that is in a plant's ideal range for nutrient uptake. The three nutrients plants require most for healthy plant growth are nitrogen (N), phosphorous (P) and potassium (K). These elements are called *primary* nutrients because plants require them in large quantities compared to other plant nutrients. They are what you see printed on every plant food and fertilizer package manufactured since the advent of moveable type. (Well, practically.) They are represented as three sets of numbers: 10-10-8 (meaning 10 percent nitrogen, 10 percent phosphorous and 8 percent potassium), for instance, or 3-10-15 or whatever the makeup of the food is. You can tell at a glance, then, the percentage of nitrogen in a plant food versus that of phosphorous and potassium.

But those aren't the *only* nutrients plants require for strong, vigorous growth. They also need calcium (Ca), magnesium (Mg) and sulfur (S). Because plants require these components in smaller quantities than nitrogen, phosphorous and potassium, they are referred to as *secondary* nutrients.

Finally, plants also utilize zinc (Zn), manganese (Mn), iron (Fe), boron (B), copper (Cu), molybdenum (Mo) and chlorine (Cl), which are required in very small amounts and are called *micronutrients*.

Whereas the three primary nutrients must periodically be added to soil in order to be available for plant use, most secondary and micronutrient deficiencies are easily corrected simply by keeping the soil at its optimum pH value.

But soil pH may also have a negative effect on plants in other ways.

Some minerals commonly found in soil can be toxic to plants in high enough concentrations. In highly acidic soils (with a low pH), aluminum and manganese can become more available to plants, meaning more plants will be susceptible to failure as a result of increased uptake of these elements.

By contrast, low pH values make calcium, phosphorous and magnesium less available to the plant — again, making the plants more likely to fail. At pH values of 6.5 and above (alkaline soils), phosphorous and most of the micronutrients become less available to plants.

It makes sense, then, to keep your plants' soil pH in the range of 5.5–6.5, where most of the nutrients your plants require for healthy growth are available to them.

Factors Affecting Soil pH

Why should you, as a container gardener, care about pH levels in soil? After all, it's not as if you're planning on going out and tilling under the back 80 to plant next year's winter wheat.

Are you?

Actually, understanding how important pH is to healthy plants can help you not only with your container gardening, but also with all areas of gardening. Besides, you may at some point want to use some garden soil in your containers, if only in those containers you intend to keep outdoors. In such a case, it would be nice to know whether the soil you're using for your outdoor potted plants is alkaline, acidic or neutral.

Which brings up a couple of questions: Where does pH come from, and how do we measure it and make adjustments to the soil for our plants' benefit?

Becky Thatcher and Her Golden Hair

Do you remember the story of Becky Thatcher, who I believe may have been Tom Sawyer's girlfriend in *The Adventures of Tom Sawyer*? Well, I don't either. But if I did, my recollection would go something like this:

Becky Thatcher had hair the color of spun gold. She wore it in a ponytail held in place by a bright red ribbon. She washed it in warm milk every evening, and she nourished it with honey. She kept it trimmed with a pair of silver metallic scissors.

Now, none of this is particularly relevant to container gardening, unless you stop to consider that every element in that tale — every single "thing" — has a pH value. Some things (hair, for example) are acidic, while other things (the scissors) are alkali. Few things in life are neutral.

It's the same with soil. Most soil comes from the gradual erosion of solid rock over the past billion years or so. Some rocks have an acidic pH, while others are more alkaline. The pH value of a soil, then, is influenced by the kinds of parent materials from which the soil was formed. That material, made of decomposed and eroded rock, determines the soil's alkalinity level. Soils formed from alkaline rocks are likely to have higher pH values than those formed from acidic rocks.

The pH level of soil is also affected by rainfall. Water passing through the soil leaches out basic nutrients such as calcium and magnesium.

These are replaced by acidic elements such as aluminum and iron. For this reason, soils formed under high rainfall conditions are more acidic than those formed under arid (dry) conditions. That's one of the reasons that the soil in the Amazonian rain forests are more acidic than those in the Mojave Desert.

Applying fertilizers rich in ammonium or urea increases the acidity of a soil. So, too, does the decomposition of organic matter (fallen leaves, rotting fruit, etc. — think rain forest again).

By contrast, the lack of these elements in soil decreases the acidity of a soil.

In short, virtually everything that comes in contact with soil affects its pH level, sometimes moving it up the pH scale and sometimes moving it down.

Increasing the Soil pH

To make soils less acidic (more alkaline), gardeners have traditionally applied a material that contains some form of alkaline lime, most often in the form of ground agricultural limestone. The finer the limestone particles, the more quickly and efficiently it raises a soil's alkalinity level. Different soils, of course, will require differing amounts of lime to change the soil's pH value significantly.

The texture of a soil, the amount of organic matter it contains and the plants you plan on growing all come into consideration when adjusting a soil's pH. Soils low in clay content, for example, require less lime than soils high in clay content to make the same pH change.[14]

To determine how much lime you should add to your soil to raise the alkalinity level, you'll need to have your soil tested. You can do this either by submitting a soil sample to a soil-testing company or your agricultural extension agent or by using a basic soil-testing kit available from your local nursery or garden center.

The ideal time for testing garden soil is late in the year before the ground freezes so that you have time to amend the soil with acid or alkali for the following year's planting. (These things often take a bit of time to work their way into and change the pH level of the soil.) If test results indicated a need for limestone, for example, you could apply it in the fall or winter, or any time up until two to three months prior to planting, in order to allow time for it to neutralize the acidity of the soil.

The most important factor determining the effectiveness of lime is placement. Maximum contact of lime with the soil is essential. Most liming materials are only slightly soluble in water, so incorporation into the soil is a must in order for the lime to affect the soil's pH level.[15]

This, of course, is bad news for lawn owners who want to adjust the pH of their soil, but it's great news for container gardeners, who can incorporate the right amount of lime into a pot full of soil with a simple garden trowel in about 60 seconds flat.

Wood Ashes

Some gardeners also use wood ashes to raise their soil's pH. Ashes contain small amounts of potassium, phosphate, boron and other trace elements. They are not as effective as limestone in raising a soil's alkalinity, but, because ashes are often plentiful and work relatively slowly and safely in changing pH, they remain a popular remedy.

One word of caution, though, for anyone using an alkali compound such as limestone or ashes: these materials are extremely caustic and need to be kept away from direct contact with young plants or plant roots as they may cause permanent damage! And always wear gloves and eye protection when working with these materials.

Decreasing the Soil pH

Many ornamental plants and some fruit plants such as blueberries require slightly to strongly acid soil. These species develop iron chlorosis when grown in soils that are too alkaline. Iron chlorosis is often confused with nitrogen deficiency because the symptoms are similar (pale, sickly looking yellow leaves). It can be corrected quickly and easily simply by reducing the soil's pH value.[16]

Two materials most often used for *lowering* a soil's pH level are aluminum sulfate and sulfur, both of which are commonly available at garden supply centers. Aluminum sulfate will change the soil pH instantly because the aluminum produces acidity as soon as it dissolves in the soil. Sulfur, on the other hand, requires some time to work, because it must first convert to sulfuric acid with the aid of certain soil-borne bacteria. The conversion rate of the sulfur depends upon several variables, including the fineness of the sulfur, the amount of moisture in the soil, soil temperature and of course the presence of the proper bacteria. The

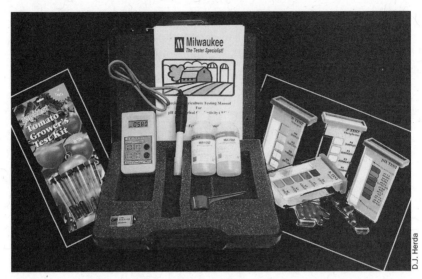

One of the quickest and easiest (if not always the most accurate) ways to have your soil tested is to do it yourself with one of a wide range of testing kits on the market.

necessity for all these factors to come into play is a vote in favor of using aluminum sulfate rather than sulfur to lower their soil's pH level.[17]

No matter which material you choose, work it into the soil thoroughly. If any of the materials come in contact with a plant's leaves, wash it off immediately to prevent leaf burn and damage to the plant. Follow directions on the package carefully.

Having Your Soil Tested

There are several ways to test your soil's pH level. The simplest is to have a soil analysis done professionally. For that, you'll need to collect 12 or more cores to be combined and tested as one. The 12 cores should include soil from the surface to a depth of 6 inches. You can use a simple *clean* garden trowel to collect the cores. As you pull the plugs from the ground, place them in a clean bucket and mix. Try not to include any cores where pesticides or fertilizers have recently been applied to avoid tainting the results. Take a minimum of two cups of this mixed sample to your county Extension office.

If you want to test different sections of your garden, repeat the process with each section. Be sure to keep track of which part of the garden each sample came from. (Testing various sections may be important if you have a large garden, where the soil could theoretically range from mildly alkaline in the northeast corner to strongly acidic in the southwest corner).

The extension officer will ask you to fill out the information on a soil test box, complete a record sheet and check the appropriate boxes for the analyses you want done. The cost of a standard soil test is approximately $6 per sample. This test provides unbiased, scientific information on the soil's pH value; the levels of phosphorous, potassium, calcium, magnesium, zinc and manganese in the soil; and fertilizer and lime recommendations (if any) for the specific plants you want to grow.

The lab will mail the results to you in from seven to fourteen days. Simple enough? If not, perhaps you'd rather run your own analysis. Here's what that entails.

Do-It-Yourself Testing

Purchase a soil-testing kit at your local nursery supply center or on the Internet. Most kits are relatively inexpensive.

To conduct your own test, simply follow the directions that come with the kit. Usually, you'll be asked to collect approximately one cup of soil from about four inches below the surface and mix that with two cups of water. As in collecting samples for a professional evaluation, be sure to use a clean gardening tools and containers to avoid contamination.

Next, you'll place the mixture in a tester, add the chemicals provided with the kit and shake well. By matching the color of the soil "soup" to a chart, you'll get a fairly reliable indication of the pH level of the soil. Other tests will tell how much nitrogen, phosphorous and potassium are in the soil, and that will give you a good idea of what kinds of fertilizers and plant foods to use when feeding your plants.

To Test or Not?

If you have had good success with a certain commercial soil mix or even with soil you have collected from your garden and don't see any need for conducting a soil test, at least be aware of these two points.

First, native soils found east of the Mississippi River (excluding Florida) are generally *acidic* in makeup and may require the addition of pelletized lime or dolomite to raise the soil's pH level, even if only slightly, to bring it to within the range that most plants enjoy, which is a pH level of 5.5–6.5, or slightly on the acidic side. Native soils found west of the Mississippi River and in Florida are generally more *alkali* and will require the incorporation of aluminum sulfate to lower the soil's pH level to something more akin to your plants' liking.

Second, some commercial potting mixes are manufactured to be either slightly acidic (toward 5.5 on the pH scale) or slightly alkaline (toward 7.5 on the scale). By matching the right pH soil to the plants you intend to grow, you can achieve the same goals you would by running a soil test and adjusting the soil to suit your plants' needs.

That's another one of the major advantages that container gardening has over backyard gardening. You call the shots. You choose which plants to grow and in which potting mixes. If you need to provide an acidic soil for your blueberry shrubs, for example, you can do so simply by purchasing the right potting mix and feeding your shrubs with an acidic plant food.

If, on the other hand, you need a more alkaline mix to satisfy the needs of another plant, you can do that just as easily in a separate pot. In that way, every plant you grow can have exactly the right pH in which to prosper with a minimum of fuss and muss on your part.

Try serving up *that* kind of room service to your typical backyard garden plants!

01:00   IN A MINUTE

- Your soil's pH level is probably the single most important element in successful container gardening.

- With very little effort, you can raise low-acidic soil pH levels and lower high-alkali soil pH levels to better suit your plants' growing requirements.

- You can have a professional lab test for your soil's pH, or you can do it yourself with a simple and inexpensive kit at home.

- Knowing what your soil is made of—and what it lacks—can save you hours of time and weeks of frustration in growing container plants for food.

Peppers (*Capsicum annuum*)

Habit: Sweet, hot, upright on a single stalk

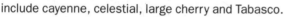

Cultivars: Although types of peppers belong in one of six groups, most are classified according to their degree of hot or mild flavor. The mild peppers include bell, banana, pimento and sweet cherry. The hot peppers include cayenne, celestial, large cherry and Tabasco. Some popular cultivars include:

- *Sweet Peppers:* Blushing Bear, Keystone Giant, Jackpot, Sweet Banana and Valencia
- *Hot Peppers:* Jalapeno, Red Chili, Giant Thai, Super Cayenne II and Hungarian Yellow Wax

Seed or Transplants: Both

Pot Size: Medium

Water: Practice good cultivation and provide adequate moisture. Water the container to provide a uniform moisture supply to the crop. Water sufficiently to moisten the soil to a depth of at least 6 inches. The critical period for moisture is during fruit set and fruit development.

Comments: Peppers are warm-season plants that grow best at temperatures of 70–85°F during the day and 60–70°F at night. They generally require a long growing season and grow very slowly during cool periods,

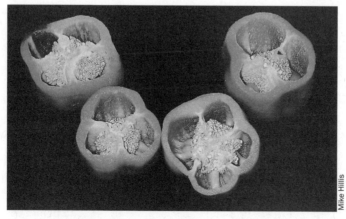

Sweet Bell Peppers (*Capsicum annuum*)

but watch them take off when the dog days of summer hit! Do not plant peppers in outdoor containers until the soil has warmed and after the last chance of frost. Start seed indoors six to eight weeks prior to transplanting.

Seeds: Plant seeds to a depth approximately twice the thickness of the seed; water and tamp soil firmly. Cover pot with a clear plastic container or wrap, and wait for germination. Keep soil moist but not saturated, and keep pot out of direct sunlight to avoid overheating. Uncover at the first sign of sprouts. Thin to approximately one plant per six square inches.

Transplants: Place in hole no deeper than original root ball, and press soil around stem firmly with fingers.

Soil: Peppers require no more than moderate amounts of fertilizer. A soil test is always the best method of determining the fertilization needs of a crop. In lieu of that, apply fertilizer in the form of 5-10-10 as recommended on the fertilizer package. Use a starter solution (half-strength the recommended fertilizer dosage) for transplants. Avoid giving your peppers too much nitrogen before they set fruit or you'll end up with all foliage. After fruits set, fertilize normally, using a complete fertilizer. Soil pH should be between 5.8 and 6.5 for best growth.

Insects: Insects that may be a problem include European corn borer, corn earworms and armyworms. **Solutions:** Spray with biologically friendly non-detergent soap mixed with water (1T per gallon water). Pick off larger pests and dispose of by hand.

Diseases: Blossom-end rot is a common problem that causes a brown to black sunken rot at the blossom end of the fruit. It is caused by a calcium deficiency. Blossom drop occurs when night temperatures are above 75°F or when a crop of fruit set is excessive. Other troublesome diseases of peppers in the container garden are bacterial wilt, bacterial leaf spot, Fusarium wilt, Pythium root rot, Cercospora leaf spot, Southern blight and anthracnose (on fruit). **Solutions:** Many disease problems can be avoided by using certified disease-free seeds and transplants. Do not use tobacco products near peppers, because tobacco mosaic virus can be readily spread from tobacco. To treat specific diseases safely, see Chapter 15.

Health Benefits: All peppers are good sources of vitamins A, C and K, but red peppers are especially good. The antioxidant vitamins A and C help to prevent cell damage, cancer and aging-related diseases while increasing the efficiency of the body's immune system. They are also potent anti-inflammatories beneficial in fighting both arthritis and asthma. Vitamin K helps to promote blood clotting, strengthen bones and protect cells from oxidation.

Red peppers are a particularly good source of the carotenoid lycopene (also found in tomatoes), which is earning a reputation for helping to prevent prostate and bladder cancers. Beta-cryptoxanthin, another carotenoid in red peppers, has shown promise for helping to prevent lung cancer related to smoking and the inhalation of second-hand smoke.

Besides being rich in phytochemicals, peppers provide a good amount of fiber.

Hot peppers, notorious for their culinary "sting," get their kick from something called capsaicin, which acts on pain receptors in the mouth. Capsaicin congregates in the white membranes of peppers, imparting its "heat" to the seeds as well. The capsaicin in hot peppers has been shown to decrease cholesterol levels and triglycerides in the blood, boost the overall immune system and reduce the risk of stomach ulcers (notwithstanding a long-held myth to the contrary) by destroying harmful bacteria in the stomach (such as H. pylori) that can lead to ulcers.

Both hot and sweet peppers contain substances that have been shown to increase the body's heat production and oxygen consumption for about 20 minutes after eating, which is great news for dieters. Increased oxygen consumption means your body is burning extra calories, aiding in weight loss and lending new credence to the phrase, "Eat yourself thin!"

Ready for the Kitchen: Peppers should be ready for harvest in about 70 to 85 days after transplanting. When starting from seed, expect 100 to 120 days to maturity. Harvest *bell peppers* when they reach full size, the fruit walls are firm and the peppers are still in the green or yellow state. Handle carefully, as the stems of pepper plants are brittle. When harvesting the fruit, cut the stems instead of pulling to avoid breaking branches. Varieties turn from green to red, yellow or chocolate when allowed to mature on the plant. Bell peppers can be left on the plant to turn color; however, they should be picked as soon as the change is complete to avoid over-ripening. *Hot peppers*, except for jalapenos, are allowed to ripen and change colors on the plant. Jalapeno peppers should be harvested when the fruits turn black-green. Yields are smaller for hot peppers. Store peppers in the refrigerator. The optimal conditions for storage are temperatures of 45–50°F with 80- to 90-percent relative humidity for two to three weeks.

Annual Savings: Approximately $48 per year per person on average.

11

Food for Thought

Coming in a close second to pH balance for the overall health of your container plants is another area where container gardeners can excel with a mere fraction of the effort required of backyard gardeners: plant nutrients.

Since nearly all planting mixes contain a certain amount of nutrients for your plants, your main concern for choosing a supplemental food is to replace those nutrients that your plants use up in their endless quest to fuel their remarkable growth engines.

There are 16 nutrient elements that are essential for the growth and reproduction of plants. Plants obtain the three most abundant of these — carbon, hydrogen and oxygen — from water and air. The remaining 13 elements are divided into three categories: primary nutrients, secondary nutrients and micronutrients.

Fertilizer Types

Fertilizers, or plant foods, may be divided into two broad groups: organic and inorganic, or synthetic (i.e., chemical). An organic fertilizer is derived from a living plant or animal source. Chemical fertilizers are usually manufactured and have the advantage of low cost.

Commonly used synthetically manufactured fertilizers are made up almost entirely of nitrogen, potassium and phosphorous — the big three — in forms that are easily accessible by plants. In contrast, organic fertilizers are more likely to have a significantly greater percentage of micronutrients, and those micronutrients are likely to be in forms that are not so readily absorbed. Nitrogen, too, is slow in availing itself to plant use in an organic fertilizer because the organic nitrogen must be reduced by microorganisms in the soil to ammonium (NH_4) and nitrate (NO_3).

Thus, inorganic fertilizers are "fast," while organic fertilizers tend to be more "time- release."[18]

Another potential drawback of organic fertilizers is that they may not release enough of their main nutrients at one time to give the plant what it needs for best growth. Because organic fertilizers depend on soil organisms to break them down to release their nutrients, most of them are effective only when soil is moist and the soil temperature is warm enough for the soil organisms to be active.

Kill off or stunt the growth of the soil organisms, and you shut down the nutrient value of the food source. Microbial activity is also influenced by soil pH and aeration, or the amount of oxygen entering the soil.[19]

On the positive side, organic fertilizers increase the soil's organic matter content and improve the soil's physical structure — something synthetic fertilizers don't do.

Oops, but here's another plus for organic fertilizers: they're less polluting to the environment. Inorganic fertilizers are often among the major sources of groundwater pollution. The nitrogen is so readily available in solution with water that it easily leaches from the point of application to end up in streams, rivers and other waterways. Although that's not much of a problem to container gardeners, something else is: Water-soluble chemical fertilizers can injure plants if allowed to remain in contact with foliage. Slow-release fertilizers, on the other hand, are less susceptible to leaching from the soil and are better to use in sandy soil, which leaches especially easily.[20]

Here's a look at three commonly available fertilizer types.

Inorganic Fertilizers: Various salts and minerals can serve as inorganic fertilizer materials. (They are inorganic because they do not come from organic matter, such as leaves, pine needles, etc.) A few examples of inorganic fertilizers are ammonium sulfate, potassium nitrate, super-phosphate, potassium chloride and potassium sulfate.

Synthetic Organic Fertilizers: These are artificially made (i.e., manufactured) organic materials used for fertilization. Two examples are urea and ureaform.

Natural Organic Fertilizers: These are naturally occurring fertilizers, which include some of the most commonly used fertilizer materials such as these:

- Cottonseed meal, a by-product of cotton manufacturing. Formulas vary slightly but generally contain 7% nitrogen, 3% phosphorous and 2% potassium (sometimes referred to as "potash"). Cottonseed meal is acidic and is often used for feeding acid-loving plants, such as azaleas, camellias, rhododendrons and blueberries.
- Blood meal, the dried, powdered blood collected from cattle slaughterhouses. It is a rich source of nitrogen, and it supplies some of the essential micronutrients for plants, including iron.
- Bone meal, the dried, powdered bones collected from cattle slaughterhouses. It is similarly a rich source of nitrogen, as well as a powerful magnet for every stray hound in the county.
- Fish emulsion, a well-rounded, general-purpose fertilizer that is a blend of partially decomposed pulverized fish. Despite its repulsive odor, it is a popular fertilizer because it feeds low levels of nutrients over a prolonged period of time. (And the smell dissipates after a few days.) Needless to say, this is not a favorite food for indoor container gardeners unless the container can be "aired out" for a couple of days before being moved inside.
- Manure. Another complete fertilizer that is low in the amounts of nutrients it can supply, manure is best used as a soil conditioner (to make tough soils more "friable") rather than as a main supplier of nutrients. It is also an effective pesticide when used properly. (See Chapter 15.)
- Sewage sludge, another recycled product, this one from municipal sewage treatment plants. It is, in effect, human waste. Two forms are commonly available, activated and composted. Activated sludge has higher concentrations of nutrients than composted sludge and is usually sold in a dry, granular form for use as a general purpose, long-lasting fertilizer. Not recommended for food crops or, for that matter, for any plants without a chemical analysis for toxins such as the heavy metal, cadmium.

Other aspects that may be of benefit to know include fertilizer analysis, ration and formulation.

Fertilizer Analysis

All fertilizers are labeled with three numbers that indicate their guaranteed analysis, or the fertilizer grade. These three numbers give the percentage by weight of nitrogen (N), phosphorous (P_2O_5) and potassium (K_2O). Often, to simplify matters, these numbers are referred to as N-P-K.

In a 100-pound bag of fertilizer labeled 10-10-10, then, there are 10 pounds each of N, P_2O_5 and K_2O.

Fertilizer Ratio

The fertilizer ratio pertains to the proportions of the three primary nutrients available in a fertilizer. For example, the ratio of 16-4-8 fertilizer is 4:1:2 or 4 parts nitrogen to 1 part phosphorous to 2 parts potassium.

This is a Martha Stewart moment (you know, "a good thing"), which can come in handy following a soil analysis, because the report you receive will advise you on how to amend your soil for the crops you intend to grow. Knowing how much of each of the primary nutrients to add — in what percentages — will help you zero in on the perfectly balanced soil for you.

Fertilizer Type

Here are a few other useful things about fertilizer types before you go out and plunk down your hard-earned cash on some relatively costly plant foods.

Complete fertilizer: A fertilizer is called "complete" when it contains each of the major plant nutrients: nitrogen, phosphorous and potassium. If plants need only one of these nutrients as indicated by the soil test report, a complete fertilizer is not called for.

Balanced fertilizer: A fertilizer is called "balanced" when it contains equal amounts of N, P_2O_5 and K_2O (nitrogen, phosphorous and potassium). A 10-10-10 fertilizer is a balanced fertilizer.

Special-purpose fertilizer: There are fertilizers packaged for certain types of plants or certain uses, such as "camellia, rhododendron and azalea food." These fertilizers belong to the "acid-loving plant foods." Some of the compounds in these fertilizers have an acidifying reaction on the soil, so they are beneficial to acid-loving plants growing in soil that is naturally neutral or alkaline in pH. Note that acid-balanced fertilizers are beneficial for all acid-loving plants and not merely the ones spelled out on the label.

Slow-release fertilizer: These fertilizers contain one or more essential elements that are released or made available to the plant over an extended period of time. This minor miracle of mankind is accomplished in one of three ways (or in combination thereof):

- Use of slowly dissolving material, such as granite meal and rock phosphate; the longer the material takes to dissolve in order to become available to the plant, the slower the release is said to be.
- Use of materials from which nitrogen is released by microorganisms in the soil.
- Use of materials coated with resin or sulfur, which controls the rate of nutrients released from the granules in the soil, often dependent once again upon the amount of moisture in the soil.

Slow-release fertilizers need not be applied as frequently as other fertilizers. Outdoor container gardeners should avoid using slow-release fertilizers on trees and shrubs in late summer and fall, because doing so could entice the plant into late-season growth. As a result, the plant may not harden-off properly in preparation for winter and may suffer severe winter damage or die off.

Fertilizer/pesticide combination: The major reason for buying a fertilizer combined with a pesticide is convenience. The problem is that the timing for a fertilizer application rarely coincides with the appearance of a specific disease or insect problem, and particularly not so in every area of the country at the same time.

Fertilizer Formulation
Fertilizers come in many shapes and sizes. The type or form the fertilizer comes in is called its formulation. Some are liquids, some are pellets,

some are granules, etc. Some of the formulations available to the home-owner include water-soluble powders, liquids, tablets, granular solids, slow-release pellets and slow-release spikes.

Federal law requires that the manufacturer guarantees what is claimed on the label. In some cases a fertilizer will contain secondary nutrients or micronutrients not listed on the label because the manufac-turer does not want to go through the additional expense of analyzing and guaranteeing the exact amounts. Regardless, you can be pretty sure that the nutrients and amounts that the manufacturer *has* listed on the label are going to be pretty accurate.

Of course, knowing what's in a plant food isn't going to help you where the timing of its application is concerned. For that you're going to have to read further down the label to the application instructions. When you do, here are a few of the things you're likely to find.

Timing of applications: Soil type plays a major role in determining when you apply a fertilizer. Loose, sandy soils require more frequent ap-plications of nitrogen and other nutrients than clay-type soils, even in pots. The reason is that water tends to leach nutrients out of sand-rich soils more quickly than from heavily loamy organic soils.

Other factors affecting frequency of application include the plants being grown, the frequency and amount of watering, the type of fertil-izer used and the rate at which the specific fertilizer is released.

Just remember that root crops, because of their very nature of grow-ing underground, require less nitrogen than do leafy crops, which need to sustain good top growth for adequate production. Also, most trees and shrubs, including those suitable for growing in containers, perform nicely either with one application of a good all-purpose fertilizer once a year or a continuous feeding of compost or manure tea at every water-ing. (See Chapter 15.)

Naturally, it pays to group plants in a single container according not only to their light and water requirements but also their nutritional needs. Placing root crops together with foliar crops may not be the best way to approach companion planting.

In the landscape, plants should be fertilized in late winter or spring. Moving plants indoors in pots may extend the growing season of perennial plants somewhat (deciduous plants are going to bloom, bear fruit and die pretty much on schedule with their outdoor brethren, regardless of indoor temperatures). Still, come winter, with its cooler temperatures and shorter days, even the hardiest perennial is going to need to rest up for the next season. That's a good time to cut back on feeding, or eliminate fertilizing altogether, in order to give the plant an opportunity to go dormant.

Fertilizing trees and shrubs after July 1 can cause them to flush with new growth on woody tissues that are normally preparing themselves for the coming winter. For outdoor container plants, this may delay dormancy, resulting in winter damage or kill. For indoor container plants, late-season fertilizing may cause the plants to become overstressed by trying to grow all year long when they're built to incorporate a rest period into their complex growth schedules.

Methods of Application

Another one of a fertilizer's application instructions concerns the methods of application. As with in-ground gardening, there are various methods of applying food to container plants, depending upon the formulation of the fertilizer and the plant's needs.

Broadcasting: A recommended rate of fertilizer is spread over the growing area and left to filter into the soil or is incorporated into the soil with a hand trowel or mini-rake. For container plants, you can sprinkle granules at the recommended rate over the surface and gently work them into the top half-inch or so of soil. Don't dig any deeper than that, or you'll run the risk of disturbing or damaging the plants' delicate root systems. Water thoroughly after broadcasting.

Starter Solutions: One of the easiest ways to fertilize container plants is to use a liquid fertilizer high in phosphorous as a starter solution for young plants. Continue its use as the plants get larger. Dilute the solution according to the directions.

Side Dressing: You can apply dry fertilizer as a side dressing after plants are up and growing well by scattering the granules or powder four to six inches from the plant's main stalk. Work it into the soil lightly and water thoroughly. Avoid planting closer to the stalk, or you may damage or even kill the plant.

Foliar Feeding: Soluble fertilizers are becoming increasingly popular for foliar fertilization, even with potted plants. These fertilizers work by absorption through the plants' leaves. They are usually applied in very weak dilutions with water, using a pressurized sprayer or trigger-pump spray. Foliar feeding is especially useful when:

- insufficient fertilizer was mixed into the soil before planting;
- you want to encourage a quick growth spurt;
- you want to bypass the micronutrients (such as iron and zinc) that are locked into the soil;
- the soil is too cold for plants to extract or use the fertilizer applied to the soil.

Foliar-applied nutrients are absorbed and used by the plant quite rapidly. While this method can give relief from nutrient deficiency symptoms, remember that it's a temporary diet at best, affecting only existing leaves and providing good results primarily in spring, when foliar growth is most rapid.

Foliar applications do not, of course, address the underlying cause of any long-term nutrient deficiency, which is generally an imbalance of

Feeding your plants can be as simple or as complicated a process as you want to make it. Just remember to use common sense and always err on the side of too little rather than too much!

the soil pH value and resulting unavailability of nutrients. Think of foliar feeding of potted plants as a quick fix to a more serious problem, and always be careful not to use too strong a solution, especially with indoor plants. They rarely enjoy the benefit of occasional rains to wash their leaves clean between feedings!

What's a Good Fertilizer to Buy?

When shopping for a good fertilizer, there are a few more things to keep in mind in order to get the most bang for your plant-food dollar.

1. For quick foliar growth, look for a fertilizer that contains most of its nitrogen in the form of nitrate, ammoniacal and/or urea forms. For long-lasting results with a low potential of leaching, shop for a fertilizer with a high percentage of water-insoluble nitrogen, which will be more expensive than the readily soluble forms. The best buy for general feeding use is a food with a combination of fast- and slow-release nitrogen.

2. Unfortunately, in shopping for plant food (as in shopping for most anything these days), you often end up paying for the brand name and the millions of advertising dollars the company uses to promote its products. Keep that in mind, watch for sales on fertilizers and buy wherever the prices are lowest.

   Also, keep in mind that a higher-analysis fertilizer such as a 16-4-8 will nearly always cost more but will cover more area than a lower-analysis food, such as a 3-2-5.

3. Remember that simply because a manufacturer chooses to market a fertilizer as specifically geared toward one plant (a "lawn" or "tomato" or "camellia" fertilizer, for example) doesn't mean that it can't be used on every growing thing you own, so long as its analysis meets your plants' requirements. Sometimes, people shy away from buying plant-specific fertilizers because they don't understand this principle and end up paying more for a major brand of general-purpose plant food.

   The exception to this rule, of course, is when a fertilizer also contains a fungicide or insecticide, which could injure certain plants while leaving others untouched. In that case, opt for the safer fertilizer. You can always worry about the insects and diseases down the road — *if* they become a problem!

01:00 IN A MINUTE

- Plants need nutrients no less than people do, and for many of the same reasons.

- Many different types of fertilizers exist, and not all are equal.

- Understanding fertilizer analysis can help you to grow bigger, healthier, more productive plants.

- Knowing when and how to fertilize is one of the keys to successful container gardening.

Onion (*Allium cepa*)
Leek (*Allium porrum*)
Shallot (*Allium ascolonicum*)
Garlic (*Allium sativum*)

Habit: Bulb

Cultivars: Numerous onion cultivars are commonly grown with good success, including:
- *Bulbing onions:* Candy, Granex (white), Stockton Sweet Red and Yellow Granex
- *Green bunching onions:* Green onions may be onions of any variety that are harvested before they bulb. The following onion varieties are especially bred for bunching: Beltsville Bunching and Evergreen Bunching

Seed or Transplants: Both

Pot Size: Medium

Water: Proper soil moisture is critical for continuous root growth and for supplying the needs of the foliage and bulb. During the growing season make sure onions have plenty of moisture, especially after bulbs begin enlarging, to assure large bulbs and better yields. A week before harvest, discontinue watering to encourage the onion to form protective scales, which will make it hardier to store.

Comments: Onions and the related shallots, leeks and garlic all grow best during cool weather and are usually planted in the fall for late spring harvest. Onion plants can also be planted in early spring for summer harvest. Leeks are planted in late summer or early fall for winter harvest. Shallots and garlic both grow best from a fall planting. All onion relatives should be grown in full sun for best results. Grow either from seed, sets (tiny immature bulbs) or transplants. The different methods vary in the season and area that they are best suited for. Plant seeds for bulb onions in the early fall. Onion sets can be planted in fall or early spring. Onions grown from transplants should be planted in the early spring for best results.

Onion (*Allium cepa*)

Seeds: Plant seeds to a depth approximately twice the thickness of the seed; water and tamp soil firmly. Cover pot with a clear plastic container or wrap, and wait for germination. Keep soil moist but not saturated, and keep pot out of direct sunlight to avoid overheating. Uncover at the first sign of sprouts. Thin to approximately one plant per six square inches.

Transplants: Place in hole no deeper than original root ball, and tamp around stem firmly with your fingers.

Soil: A fertile, well-drained, loamy soil with plenty of organic matter is best for growing quality onions (and most root crops, for that matter). Clay soils often produce a hotter onion, while sandy soils require more fertilizer and water than loamy soils. The ideal pH is between 6.0 and 6.5.

Insects: The most damaging insect pests of onions are the onion maggot, which feeds on the bulbs, and onion thrips, which suck sap from the leaves. Onion maggots are attracted to decomposing organic matter. Good sanitation is necessary to avoid maggots. **Solutions:** Spray with biologically friendly non-detergent soap mixed with water (1T per gallon).

Diseases: Diseases are seldom a problem with container onions. Good cultural practices will help prevent disease. Never plant onions in the same soil more often than once every four years. Plant in well-drained soil. **Solutions:** To avoid storage diseases, be sure onions are well-cured before storing.

Health Benefits: Onions, like garlic, shallots and leeks, are members of the *Allium* family. All are good sources of the sulfur-containing compounds that produce the strong odors that some people find objectionable. They are also responsible for most of the health-promoting effects of these bulbs. Onions contain allyl propyl disulphide, while garlic is rich in allicin, diallyl disulphide, diallyl trisulfide and other compounds. Onions are also rich in the trace mineral, chromium, that helps cells respond to insulin, making them useful to diabetics. They also contain vitamin C and numerous flavonoids, especially quercetin.

Renowned over the years for their beneficial effects on diabetics, onions deserve full credit and more. Experiments have shown that allyl propyl disulfide competes with insulin, which is also a disulphide, to occupy the sites in the liver where insulin is inactivated. The result is an increase in the amount of insulin available to usher glucose into cells, resulting in the lowering of blood sugar.

Onions are also among a small number of fruits and vegetables that have contributed to a significant reduction in heart disease risk as seen in a meta-analysis of seven prospective studies. Of the more than 100,000 individuals who participated in the studies, those whose diets included onions, tea, apples and broccoli (the richest sources of flavonoids) experienced a 20 percent reduction in the risk of heart disease. As a bonus, both onions and garlic help to lower the risk of cancer, increase overall bone health and promote gastrointestinal well-being.[21]

Ready for the Kitchen: Pull bulb onions when about three-fourths of the tops have fallen over, usually from 90–150 days from seed. Remove tops by cutting 1–1½ inches above the top of the bulb. Thoroughly air-dry bulbs in a shaded area before storage. Keep the dry bulbs in shallow boxes or mesh bags in a cool, well-ventilated place to discourage mold growth. Ideal conditions are between 45°F and 55°F, with 50–60 percent humidity.

Harvest green onions when tops are 6 to 8 inches tall. Store them in a plastic bag in the refrigerator for up to two weeks.

Harvest leeks when they are an inch or more in diameter. Leeks will keep for several weeks in a refrigerator.

Harvest shallots for use as green onions 60 days after planting, or in the late spring after the tops have died down completely for dry bulbs. Cure bulbs in a warm, dry place for about a week.

Harvest garlic when the leaves begin to yellow in early summer. Lift up the entire plant by hand or with a spading fork, being careful not to bruise the bulbs. Brush off the soil but do not wash the bulbs. Cure in a warm, shady place with good air movement. Hang in bundles or spread as a single layer on screens or drying racks. Allow bulbs to dry until the neck is dry and the outer skin is papery, approximately two to three weeks. Remove tops when dry and store by braiding or tying several heads together and hanging up or by cutting tops off and placing bulbs in a mesh bag. Most varieties will keep for six to eight months in a well-ventilated, cool, dry area.

Annual Savings: Approximately $45–$80 per year per person on average, depending upon use.

Cultivars, Hybrids and Varietals

Okay, now you're ready. You understand what's going on here. You know all about the benefits of container gardening. You get the economics of it. You know where to find the pots you're going to need and how to make your own when necessary. You understand the whole soil-pH level-nutrients deal.

Now the only question is, where do you go from here?

The answer: Why, to the nursery, of course.

And what will you find there?

I'm glad you asked.

At one time in horticultural history, we had plants. Period. We had some tomatoes and we had some peas, and we had some corn and some rutabaga and some blueberries and some squash and some melons and some zucchini and a few more things to stick our forks into.

Today, we have all of those and 50 times more. A hundred times more. A thousand!

The reason?

Cultivars. Hybrids. Varietals.

In her wisdom over the years, it seems that Mother Nature wasn't content with giving the universe corn. No, she had to give the universe corn 1, corn 2, corn 3, corn 4 and so forth, ad infinitum.

As if that weren't enough, humankind, when it eventually made its appearance on earth to begin scratching around for a free meal, determined that, if Mother Nature could mess with plants, so could we.

And so we have.

The results are even *more* different human-produced cultivars, hybrids and varietals of even more different fruits and vegetables (not to mention ornamentals) than you could ever imagine.

But what, exactly, are cultivars, hybrids and varietals? Let's take a look.

The Same Difference

The word *cultivar* is a contraction of the words "cultivated variety." It refers to plants within the same species that are bred with distinct characteristics.

Some cultivars gain popularity because they are particularly pest resistant or because they have the ability to survive in certain climates unique among the species. Other cultivars are valued simply for their beauty or fragrance — roses, for example. The horticultural industry continually reinvents itself by creating new cultivars.

Cultivar names are designated with single quotes, such as Sedum 'Autumn Joy.'

A *hybrid* is a cross between two different plant varieties to get the desired attributes of each. Hybrids are developed for disease resistance, size of bloom, time in bloom, color, taste or any other reason a plant might be considered special or unique.

Since hybrids are a cross between varieties, the seed produced by hybrids will not usually produce a plant similar to it. For this reason, plants grown from hybrid seeds are said to be *untrue*.

Seedlings grown from a hybrid *could* exhibit some of the traits of one or both parent plants, but it could also be something totally different.

With patience (and we're talking years here — far more patience than I have been willing to exhibit), hybrid seeds can be selected carefully and grown out until they eventually stabilize and begin growing true to the parent hybrid. However, most seed companies simply continue cross breeding to produce the seed, since doing so is less costly, quicker and more reliable.

Varietals is another name for cultivars — that is, they are plants within the same species that are bred to produce distinctive desirable characteristics.

So, when you set out on your search to find the best candidates for growing in containers, you can go armed with the knowledge that cer-

A wide range of cultivars and hybrids are introduced each year, many of them ideal candidates for container gardening. Experiment to find the ones you enjoy the most.

tain plant characteristics have been bred into some plants and out of others. Certain plants have been cultivated to produce disease-resistant varieties, for example, or smaller, more-compact growing habits better suited to container gardening or greater fruit yields.

You may find yourself wondering what variety or which hybrid to choose based upon the hundreds of thousands on the market, with new plant cultivars making their introductions every new growing season.

Or you may decide to go in an entirely different direction.

One More Consideration

There is one other classification of plant you might find worth considering for your container garden. It's called an heirloom plant because it is the original, naturally occurring, untampered with, unfettered, undiluted, unmanipulated, *un-everything-erated* plant species, with no single quotes around it.

These plants are often passed along from one generation to the next (thus the reference) by a gardener collecting seeds from the mature plant at harvest time. For the seeds to bear true to species, the plant must be open pollinated (OP). In other words, the plant has to be capable of producing seeds that will generate seedlings identical to the parent plant. Not all plants do this, as we have seen with cultivars and hybrids.

While plants can cross-pollinate in nature (when a bee moves from one variety to another, for example, accidentally cross-pollinating the second plant), and while hybrids repeatedly selected and grown may eventually stabilize and begin producing seed true to breed, many hybrid seeds are relatively new crosses.

Every spring, for example, the seed catalogs feature new tomato varieties — each one boasting some benefit not previously seen in other varieties. They may be labeled as hybrids or F1, which refers to the first filial generation (first-generation hybrid), or F2.

Although these hybrids may eventually stabilize, they cannot be relied upon to do so in any set period of time. The 'Early Girl' variety of tomato, for example, has been around for decades, yet the plant still cannot be induced to produce seeds that can be relied upon to have the same characteristics that you expect in an 'Early Girl' tomato. Talk about stubborn!

Because seeds from hybridized plants tend to revert to the dominant characteristics of the parents (you remember high school genetics class?), tomatoes such as 'Early Girl' grown from seeds saved from last year might be sweet and tasty — but not nearly so early.

Because of the vagaries of such behavior, many gardeners are turning toward growing heirloom plants — plants that *can* be relied upon to produce true to breed from seed year after year. As a bonus, some gardeners insist that heirlooms are hardier and more flavorful than many modern cultivars.

It stands to reason. 'Big Boy' tomatoes, originally bred to produce exceptionally large fruit, are renowned to be bland tasting. The heirlooms from which the hybrid was created are undoubtedly more flavorful; so, if you're willing to give up size for taste (and many gardeners are!), it makes sense to turn the clock back to the original 'Big Boy' parents and plant the heirloom.

Planting heirlooms also helps to assure that the continuing genetic pool of original plants remains available to future cross-breeders. Sadly, over the years, many heirlooms have been lost to the pages of antiquity simply because they had the misfortune to fall out of vogue in favor of more popular and flashy cultivars.

It's undeniably true that, as a container gardener, you're not going to find a huge percentage of heirloom plants appealing. Many are sprawling and unruly in size and growth habit; others are sturdy of stock but puny of produce. Still others require too much light or root space to be practical candidates for growing in containers or are intolerant of too much sun or shade.

But don't categorically rule out heirloom plants because there are other plants that are apparently better suited for container gardening. Just because a tomato plant grows to a compact size and shape and enjoys crowded roots doesn't mean it's the right variety for you. Experiment, read about all different heirlooms and varietals; check out the latest cultivars available from your favorite nursery source; learn all you can about the plants you're considering growing; and only then jump in with both feet.

You'll be glad you took the extra time and effort to do so.

01:00   IN A MINUTE

- Cultivars are plants within the same variety bred for different characteristics; hybrids are plants from different varieties bred for the same purpose.

- Heirloom plants are naturally occurring, unadulterated varieties that are often popular because of their hardiness.

- To find the best variety of plant for your growing needs, do some research and plant, plant and plant some more.

Spinach (*Spinacia oleracea*)

Habit: Leaf

Cultivars: Most spinach that is grown in containers is the semi-Savoy type. The Savoy characteristic refers to the amount of leaf crinkle in the plant. Slow-bolting is an important varietal characteristic for over-wintered and spring plantings (bolting refers to the forming of a flower stalk, which steals energy from the development of the fruit or—as in the case of spinach—the foliage). Resistance to downy mildew is another important characteristic in a spinach variety. Two of the best cultivars include:

- Melody and Space

Spinach (*Spinacia oleracea*)

Seed or Transplants: Both

Pot Size: Small to medium

Water: Water the container to provide a uniform moisture supply to a depth of about 6 inches. Water early so that the foliage dries before dark. Spinach requires frequent watering in order to produce a high-quality crop which, not surprisingly, is comprised of a high percentage of water. Funny how Mother Nature works.

Comments: Spinach is a hardy, cool-season crop that can be planted in early spring or fall in pots indoors or out. It makes a good patio plant, since it can survive temperatures of 20°F without injury and go right on growing.

Seeds: Plant seeds to a depth approximately twice the thickness of the seed; water and tamp soil firmly. Cover pot with a clear plastic container or wrap, and wait for germination. Keep soil moist but not saturated, and keep pot out of direct sunlight to avoid overheating. Uncover at the first sign of sprouts. Thin to approximately one plant per six square inches.

Transplants: Place in hole no deeper than original root ball and tamp around stem firmly with your fingers.

Soil: Spinach grows well in a variety of soils, but it prefers a fertile sandy loam high in organic matter. Maintain a soil pH between 5.8 and 6.5 for optimal fertility levels. Soil pH is important in growing spinach. If limestone is recommended as a result of a soil test, incorporate the lime into the planting area at least three months prior to planting. Proper watering and the use of calcium nitrate as a side dressing will discourage blackheart and tip burn, which are calcium-deficiency disorders.

Insects: Insects that may be a problem in growing spinach include aphids, cutworms, cabbage loopers, corn earworms and diamondback moth caterpillars. Aphids are a major problem because they transmit viruses to the plants. **Solutions:** Spray for aphids with biologically friendly non-detergent soap mixed with water (1T per gallon water). Pick off and destroy larger insects.

Diseases: The primary disease problems with this crop are downy mildew, white rust and seedling damping-off. **Solutions:** Keep leaves free from water overnight, and apply appropriate natural fungicide. (See Chapter 15.)

Health Benefits: Spinach is one of the healthiest of all vegetables (Popeye knew what he was talking about!) and is loaded with calcium, dietary fiber, iron, manganese, magnesium, niacin, phosphorous, potassium, riboflavin, selenium, thiamin, vitamin A, vitamin B6, vitamin C and zinc — and it has no cholesterol! All this makes it an excellent vegetable to harvest and consume year-round. In fact, if you're health-conscious, you'll get into the habit of using fresh spinach in your salads in place of lettuce. In addition to being healthier for you, it actually tastes more flavorful.

Popeye may have eaten spinach for strength, but he should have been eating it for other reasons, such as its remarkable protective qualities versus osteoporosis, heart disease, colon and other cancers, arthritis and additional diseases. Researchers have identified at least 13 different flavonoid compounds in spinach that work together as antioxidants and anticancer agents. Studies have shown that spinach extracts slow down cell division in stomach cancer cells (gastric adenocarcinomas), reduce the occurrence of skin cancers and lower the incidence of breast cancer in women.

A carotenoid found in spinach and other green leafy vegetables fights human prostate cancer two different ways, according to research published in the *Journal of Nutrition*.[22] The carotenoid called neoxanthin not only induces prostate cancer cells to self-destruct but also is converted in the intestines into additional compounds, called neochromes. These unique compounds put prostate cancer cells into a state of stasis, or rest, thus preventing their replication and the spread of the disease.

In addition to functioning as a powerful anti-carcinogenic, the high level of vitamin K in spinach helps to promote healthy bones and prevent diseases such as osteoporosis. Spinach is good for the heart, as well, because its high levels of vitamins C and A plus beta-carotene work as antioxidants to reduce the concentration of free radicals in the body.

Spinach is also an excellent source of folate, which the body needs in order to convert a potentially harmful chemical called homocysteine into

benign molecules. Homocysteine can lead to heart attack or stroke if the
levels get too high.

Spinach is an excellent source of magnesium, which is useful in lowering high blood pressure and protecting against heart disease. A typical portion of spinach salad may have a beneficial effect on blood pressure in as
short a period of time as two hours. As if that weren't enough, spinach is
also beneficial in promoting gastrointestinal health and working as an anti-
inflammatory.

If you're beginning to believe that all these benefits make Popeye
a pretty smart guy, you can attribute that to this wonder green, as well.
Researchers have found that spinach may help protect the brain from
oxidative stress while reducing the effects of brain decline in people of
advancing years. Eating only three servings of any combination of spinach, yellow vegetables and crucifers each day could slow the development of dementia by 40 percent, according to one study in the medical
journal *Neurology*.[23] The bottom line is that, if you remember to enjoy at
least three servings of these vegetables a day, you are much more likely to
remember a wide range of other things, as well!

Finally, spinach, which is rich in lutein, a carotenoid, provides effective
protection against eye diseases such as age-specific macular degeneration and cataracts (as do kale and broccoli). Since lutein, like other carotenoids, is fat-soluble and cannot be absorbed unless fat is present in the
digestive system, it's a good idea to eat a little healthy oil, such as coconut
or olive oil, with your spinach, whether fresh, sautéed or steamed. Topping
off with a hard-boiled egg (which is also rich in lutein as well as in the fats,
cholesterol and choline, will only maximize this green's positive healthful
effects.[24]

Ready for the Kitchen: Spinach should be ready to harvest in about 37–45
days after planting. Harvest dark-green tender leaves that are three to six
inches long by picking individual leaves or cutting with garden shears. Start
by picking the outer leaves and harvest the newer leaves as they reach the
desired size, thus keeping the spinach in production for weeks. Remove
the petioles (leaf stems) if they are too large and fibrous, or cook them to
soften. Rinse the spinach and dry with paper towels or a salad spinner.
Store spinach in open plastic bags in the refrigerator.

Annual Savings: Approximately $39 per year per person on average.

More than Just a Pretty Face: Companion Planting

Okay, you've gone to your favorite plant store, purchased those fruits and vegetables you want to grow this year, picked up a few seed packs for those you couldn't find as plantlets; and you're ready to put all your goodies into their respective containers.

You have a great-looking twelve-inch pot ready to plant with a really healthy-looking six-inch tomato. You put the tomato right in the center of the pot and fill the pot with soil nearly to the top.

But, wait a minute. What are you going to do next?

I mean, why does it look so...barren?

The Buddy System

Enter *companion planting*. Simply speaking, companion planting is providing a buddy for your favorite plants.

What ego! you say. What esoteric tommyrot. Why on earth would anyone be so vain as to feel the need to dress up a potted plant with more potted plants? Isn't a plant in every pot nearly as good an idea as a chicken? Isn't the false notion that if one is good, two are better, enough reason to pass?

Well, not exactly. You see, companion planting — while it can and nearly always does spruce up a container visually — is more than mere cosmetics. Science has shown over the years that, when you grow two or three different plant species together, you might actually be doing *all* of the plants a favor.

That's right.

If one plant can grow well in a large clay pot, two might just grow better. And three could possibly grow even better still, despite the increased competition for food and water.

How can this be, you ask? Pay attention, now. I want to say this only once.

Some plants, just as some people, do better in groups of mixed progeny. They grow faster, healthier, more vigorous and more resistant to diseases and pests than single-species plantings. Beans and tomatoes do well when planted together, for example, as do cucumbers and corn. Marigolds and tomatoes are stalwart buddies, as are hot peppers and French lavender.

But growing tomatoes with cucumbers? Uh-uh. Don't try it, punk. Mixing potatoes with carrots? Go ahead: make their day.

See what I mean?

Some plants, you might say, are more social with some species of plants than they are with others. Pretty much the way your Great Aunt Martha used to be. Remember the fireworks that resulted whenever she got together with your second cousin Ferne?

Science Has an Explanation

It's true. Over the years, numerous horticultural studies have been conducted to attempt to show which plants do best with which other plants and which should never be planted together. Those same studies and others have also tried to explain the rationale behind the success of companion planting. In other words: *Why*?

Botanists have known for years that many plants have natural substances in their roots, flowers, leaves or stems that can alternately repel (anti-feedants) and/or attract (pro-feedants) insects. In some situations they can also help enhance the growth rate and flavor of different varieties and species.

Hundreds of years of growing experience have shown that using companion planting throughout the landscape — as well as in containers — can be an important part of integrated pest management. While worrying about insect attacks may not be a problem when growing container plants indoors, worrying about fungus and bacterial attacks is another matter.

In effect, companion planting can help bring a more balanced eco-system to your container garden by giving Mother Nature a gentle nudge. After all, plants growing in the wild rarely grow specific to a single species. Rather, they grow among many different species, most of which are ideally suited to perform in a symbiotic relationship with their brethren.

Think of it in these terms. Nature melds a wide range of plants, in-sects, animals and other organisms into every ecosystem. They are all inter-related, because they are designed to feed off of one another, to benefit from one another in some way. In simple terms: a tree grows an apple. A person picks and eats the apple, discarding the core. The core, which contains the apple's seeds, generates a new tree in a new location, and the cycle begins anew, ad infinitum.

If you remove one element from this basic equation, you greatly re-duce the chance of apples surviving the millennium. Remove the tree, and the apple disappears. Remove the man, and the reproductive rate of apple trees is greatly diminished. You get the picture.

Add to this equation the simple premise that the death of one organ-ism can create food — not to mention new life — for another, and you be-gin to see the symbiotic relationship of all living things.

Farmers often plant soy beans or winter wheat during the "off" sea-son, only to till them under before planting their spring corn. The re-sults? The nitrogen-rich wheat or beans tilled under in spring feed the nitrogen-gobbling corn in a relationship that ultimately benefits both plants.

This is the value of companion planting in a nutshell. One plant helps the others to survive.

In the case of growing fruit and vegetables in pots, the plant we want to benefit the most from companion planting is, of course, the one we salivate over eating the most. Toward that goal, companion planting is a holistic concept due to the many intricate levels in which it works within the ecological scope of being.

By taking advantage of companion planting, gardeners can discour-age harmful pests without losing beneficial allies. Other groupings help to encourage greater fruiting and generally healthier plants. Still others encourage beneficial bacterial growth in the soil, which is beneficial to every plant's well-being.

A companion gardener harvests green onions from a container containing cabbage (a natural pairing) and marigolds, which help to repel all kinds of pests.

Now, combine these benefits with the additional beauty that companion planting can bring to your pots (marigolds and zinnias mixed with tomato plants, for example), and you begin to see a whole range of advantages.

Some Natural Companions

Here are a few naturally beneficial companion plants that do better grown together than separately.

Alfalfa is a perennial plant with deep roots. As with legumes, it is valuable for its ability to fix the soil with nitrogen while it accumulates iron, magnesium, phosphorous and potassium; so it's a good companion plant for anything requiring lush green top growth. It withstands droughts with its long taproot and can improve just about any container soil.

Asparagus is a good companion for dill, coriander, tomatoes, parsley, basil, comfrey and marigolds. Avoid: Onions, garlic and potatoes.

Basil does well when planted with tomatoes (and it's no slouch when cooked with them, either!) in order to improve both growth and flavor. It also flourishes with peppers, oregano, asparagus and petunias. As a bonus, basil repels flies and mosquitoes. That means it should be on your list of friendly plants. Do not plant near rue or sage.

Beans enrich the soil with nitrogen fixed from the air. In general, they provide good company for carrots, celery, chard, corn, eggplant, peas, potatoes, the brassicas (such as cabbage, etc.), beets, radish, strawberries and cucumbers. Beans are great for heavy nitrogen users such as corn and grain plants because beans fix nitrogen from the air into the soil so that the nitrogen used up by the corn and grains is replaced at the end of the season when the bean plants die back. French Haricot beans, sweet corn and melons have long proven to make good combinations. Summer savory deters bean beetles and improves growth and flavor. Keep beans away from the alliums (the onion family).

Borage is a great companion plant for tomatoes, squash, strawberries and most other plants. It deters tomato hornworms and cabbage worms and is one of the best bee- and wasp-attracting plants, which makes it beneficial in pollinating your outdoor container plants. It adds trace minerals to the soil and makes a good addition to the compost pile. The leaves contain vitamin C and are rich in calcium, potassium and mineral salts. Borage may benefit any plant it is growing next to by increasing resistance to pests and disease. Cut and dried, it also makes a nourishing mulch for most plants. Borage and strawberries help each other grow pest-free. Strawberry farmers frequently set a few plants in their beds to enhance the flavor and yield of their berries. Plant near tomatoes to improve growth and disease resistance, as well. After you have planted this annual once, it will come back the following season from self-seeding. Borage flowers are edible and make an attractive-looking complement to cool summer drinks such as lemonade, wine coolers and iced tea. Use in martinis at your own risk.

Cabbage does well when planted with celery, dill, onions and potatoes. Celery in particular enjoys improved growth and health, and clover inter-planted with cabbage has been shown to reduce the native cabbage aphid and cabbageworm populations by interfering with the colonization of the pests and increasing the number of predatory ground beetles. Plant chamomile with cabbage in order to improve the growth and

flavor. Be aware, though, that cabbage does not get along with strawberries, tomatoes, peppers, eggplants, rue, grapes and pole beans. Don't ask
me why.

Coriander repels aphids, spider mites and the potato beetle. A tea
from this can be used as a spray for spider mites. It's also an efficient part-
ner for anise, and the seeds are beneficial in aiding digestion.

Garlic, when planted near roses, repels aphids. It also benefits apple
trees, pear trees, cucumbers, peas, lettuce and celery. Garlic accumulates
sulfur, a naturally occurring fungicide that will help to discourage disease in the garden. Garlic is systemic in action as it is taken up by the
plants through their pores. Garlic tea used as a soil drench is taken up by
the plants' roots. In addition to being healthful for human consumption,
garlic provides a great deal of value in offending codling moths, Japanese
beetles, root maggots, snails and carrot root fly. Researchers have observed that time-released garlic capsules planted at the bases of fruit
trees actually keep deer away, although this may not be an important factor for consideration if you live in downtown Manhattan. Concentrated
garlic sprays have been observed to repel and kill whiteflies, aphids and
fungus gnats among others with as little as a 6–8 percent concentration!
It is safe for use on orchids too, and it keeps away vampires.

Kohlrabi may be planted with cucumber, onion and chives. It and
beets are perfect to grow with one another, but don't intermix it with
pole beans, peppers, strawberries or tomatoes.

Leeks can be used near apple trees, carrots, celery and onions, which
will improve their growth. They also repel carrot flies. Avoid planting
near legumes, which include peas and beans.

Lettuce does well when planted with beets, bush beans, pole beans,
cabbage, carrots, cucumbers, onions, radishes and strawberries. It grows
happily in the shade of young sunflowers.

Marigolds (*Calendula*) are a great pest deterrent. They aid in keeping soil free of nematodes and are alleged to discourage many undesirable insects. Plant freely throughout your container garden. Note,
though, that the marigolds you choose must be a scented variety for
them to work. One downside is that marigolds do attract spider mites
and slugs.

French Marigold (*T. patula*) has roots that exude a substance that
spreads in their immediate vicinity, killing nematodes. For nematode

control, plant a dense thicket of them. Some studies also show that this nematode-killing effect lasts for several years after the plants are grown. Marigolds also help to deter whiteflies when planted around tomatoes and can be used in greenhouses for the same purpose. Whiteflies hate the smell of marigolds. Do not plant French marigolds next to bean plants.

Mexican Marigold (*T. minuta*) is the most powerful of the insect-repelling marigolds and may also overwhelm weed roots such as bind weed. It supposedly repels the Mexican bean beetle and wild bunnies with otherwise voracious appetites (a problem even for outdoor container gardeners). Be careful when using it around beans and cabbage, however, as it can have a herbicidal effect.

Marjoram is a popular herb that, as a companion plant, improves the flavor of vegetables and the intensity of other herbs. Sweet marjoram is the most commonly grown type.

Melons do well when planted with corn, pumpkins, radishes and squash. Other candidates for inter-planting include marigold (to deter beetles), nasturtium (to deter insects, including some beetles) and oregano (for general pest protection).

Mint deters white cabbage moths, ants, rodents, flea beetles, fleas and aphids and improves the health of cabbage and tomatoes. Use cuttings as a mulch around members of the brassica family. It attracts hover-flies and predatory wasps, which is good. Earthworms are also attracted to mint plantings. Be careful where you plant it, though, as mint is an incredibly invasive perennial, and its seeds can fall from a potted plant to spread outdoors throughout the garden. Keep well insulated from fertile soil! Some gardeners insist that placing mint (fresh or dried) where mice are a problem is very effective in driving the destructive rodents off, although I have never found that to be true.

Nasturtium can be planted as a barrier around tomatoes, cabbage and cucumbers and under fruit trees. This attractive edible plant deters wooly aphids, whiteflies, squash bugs, cucumber beetles and other pests fond of attacking the cucurbit (cucumber) family. It makes a great "trap crop" for aphids (in particular, black aphids), which are drawn to it (especially the yellow varieties) to the benefit of more valuable crops. Nasturtium enjoys poor soil with low moisture and little or no fertilizer. Some farmers plant nasturtium within the root zone of fruit trees, which allows the trees to take up the pungent odor of the plants in order to repel bugs. It is among the best of all plants at attracting predatory insects, such as mantises, lacewings and ladybugs. It has no taste effect on fruit grown nearby. A nice variety to grow is Alaska, with its attractive green-and-white variegated leaves. The leaves, flowers and seeds of nasturtiums are all edible and make a healthy addition to nearly any salad. Do not plant near cauliflower.

Onions do well around chamomile and summer savory, improving their flavor. Other desirable companions include carrots, leeks, beets, kohlrabi, strawberries, brassicas, dill, lettuce and tomatoes. Intercropping onions and leeks with carrots confuses carrot and onion flies (it's not difficult to do), while planting onions with strawberries help the berries fight disease. Keep onions away from peas, asparagus and your fiancé.

Peas fix nitrogen in the soil. Plant next to nitrogen-heavy feeders such as corn. Companions for peas are bush beans, pole beans, carrots, celery, chicory, corn, cucumbers, eggplant, parsley, early potatoes, radishes, spinach, strawberries, sweet peppers and turnips. Do not plant with onions.

Peppers, bell (sweet) should be planted near tomatoes, parsley, basil, geraniums, marjoram, lovage, petunias and carrots. Onions make an excellent companion plant for peppers, which also grow well with okra. The okra shelters the pepper plants' brittle stems from wind damage. Don't plant them near fennel or kohlrabi, and keep them away from apricot trees because a fungus to which the pepper is prone can damage the trees. Peppers can double as ornamentals, so tuck some into your flowerbeds and borders.

Peppers (hot) have roots that exude a substance that prevents fusarium diseases, one of the prime killers of young plantlets grown from seed. Plant hot peppers anywhere you have these problems. Teas made from hot peppers can be useful as insect sprays. Hot peppers like to be grouped with cucumbers, eggplant, escarole, tomatoes, okra, Swiss chard and squash. Herbs to plant near them include basil, oregano, parsley and rosemary.

Potatoes do well with bush beans, most members of the brassicas, carrots, celery, corn, dead nettle, flax, horseradish, marigolds, peas, petunias and onions. Protect them from scab by placing comfrey leaves in with your potato sets at planting time. Horseradish, planted at the corners of the potato patch, provides general protection. Keep potatoes and tomatoes apart, since they are both susceptible to early and late blights and can cross-contaminate one another.

Radishes, one of the gardener's unsung heroes, get along well with beets, bush beans, pole beans, carrots, chervil, cucumbers, lettuce, melons, nasturtiums, parsnips, peas, spinach and members of the squash family. Radishes planted with squash plants may help protect the plants from squash borers. Radishes are also a deterrent against cucumber beetles and rust flies. Chervil and nasturtiums improve radish growth and flavor. Planting them around corn and letting them go to seed will also help deter corn borers. Chinese Daikon and Snow Belle radishes are favorites of flea beetles, which can act as lures to keep the insects away from your broccoli. Radishes are also an attractant for leafminers, which can help keep your spinach free from attack. The damage the leafminers do to radish leaves doesn't keep the root crops from maturing, which turns out to be a winning combination. Keep radishes clear of hyssop, cabbage, cauliflower, Brussels sprouts and turnips.

Spinach should be planted with peas and beans as they provide a source of natural shade for the leaf crop. Spinach also grows well with cabbage, cauliflower, celery, eggplant, onions, strawberries and radishes.

Strawberries have found great buddies in beans, borage, lettuce, onions, spinach and thyme. They don't get along well with cabbage, broccoli, Brussels sprouts, cauliflower and kohlrabi, though. Borage strengthens strawberries' resistance to insects and disease, while thyme helps to deter slugs.

Summer savory can be planted with beans and onions to improve growth and flavor while helping to repel cabbage moths, Mexican bean beetles and black aphids. As a bonus, honey bees (Mother Nature's greatest natural pollinators) love it.

Tomatoes have numerous allies, including asparagus, basil, beans, carrots, celery, chives, cucumbers, garlic, head lettuce, marigolds, mint, nasturtiums, onions, parsley, peppers, marigolds and sow thistle. One drawback with tomatoes and carrots: tomato plants can stunt the growth of your carrots, although the carrots' flavor is unaffected. Basil repels flies and mosquitoes while improving your tomatoes' growth and flavor. Bee balm, chives and mint all help to improve health and flavor. Borage deters tomato worm while spurring growth. Dill, until mature, improves growth and health, although mature dill retards tomato growth. Go figure. Also, don't plant tomatoes with corn, as both are attacked by the same worm. Similarly, avoid planting tomatoes with potatoes, as both are susceptible to early and late blight and can contaminate one another. Avoid planting with kohlrabi, which can stunt tomato growth, and don't plant near walnut trees, which increase the chances for your tomatoes to get walnut wilt.

Yarrow, a strongly scented herb, has potent insect-repelling qualities. As a bonus, it makes an excellent natural fertilizer. A handful or two of yarrow leaves added to the compost pile will help speed up decomposition. Yarrow is also beneficial for attracting predatory wasps and ladybugs. It may help to increase the essential oil content of herbs when planted among them.

01:00   IN A MINUTE

- Some plants grow better in combination with others, although not all plants make good pot partners.

- While some companion plants are natural insect or disease repellants, others are simply attractive to the eye.

- Companion planting can bring a more balanced ecosystem to your container garden while helping to boost your fruit and vegetable yields.

Broccoli (*Brassica oleracea*, Italica group)

Habit: Upright

Cultivars: There are several popular cultivars of broccoli, including:
- Packman, Everest, Premium Crop and Southern Comet, similar to Packman.

Seed or Transplants: Both

Pot Size: Medium

Water: Water the container to provide a uniform moisture supply to a depth of about 6 inches. Water early so that the foliage dries before dark.

Broccoli requires a uniform supply of moisture to produce a high-quality crop which, like spinach, is comprised of a high percentage of water.

Comments: Broccoli is a cool-season vegetable that prefers average temperatures of 65–75°F for best growth. Crops will "bolt" (produce a flower stalk) if exposed to a prolonged cold period of ten or more days of continuous temperatures between 35°F and 50°F following a favorable growing period. The larger the plants are at the time of exposure to the cold period, the higher the chance of bolting, which is the plant's natural means of propagating itself. When planted in the spring, broccoli must be planted early enough to ensure that it is harvested before temperatures become too hot.

Broccoli (*Brassica oleracea*, Italica group)

Seeds: Plant seeds to a depth approximately twice the thickness of the seed; water and tamp soil firmly. Cover pot with a clear plastic container or wrap, and wait for germination. Keep soil moist but not saturated, and keep pot out of direct sunlight to avoid overheating. Uncover at the first sign of sprouts. Thin to approximately one plant per six square inches.

Transplants: Place in hole no deeper than original root ball and tamp around stem firmly with your fingers.

Soil: Soils that are well suited for growing broccoli are fertile, well-drained and with a texture ranging from sandy loam to clay loam. Soil pH is very important and should be kept between 5.8 and 6.5 for best growth.

Insects: Insect problems include imported cabbageworm, cabbage loopers, diamondback moth larva, corn earworm and cabbage aphids. Flea beetles can severely damage small seedlings. It is important to control the insects before the heads start to develop. **Solutions:** Spray for aphids with biologically friendly non-detergent soap mixed with water (1T per gallon water). Pick off and destroy larger insects.

Diseases: Most diseases are not usually very serious on broccoli, except for black rot. Other disease problems include downy mildew, bacterial head rot and soft rot. **Solutions:** Keep leaves free from water overnight, and apply natural fungicide as required. (See Chapter 15.)

Health Benefits: As with other cruciferous vegetables, broccoli contains the phytonutrients and the indoles that have significant cancer-fighting properties. The *indole-3-carbinol* compound helps to deactivate a dangerous estrogen metabolite (4-hydroxyestrone) that encourages tumor growth, especially in estrogen-sensitive breast cells. It also increases the level of 2-hydroxyestrone, a form of estrogen that can offer similar protection against cancer, making broccoli one of the best breast cancer tools in the gardener's arsenal. It has proven equally effective in fighting a wide range of other cancers, as well.

New research has greatly advanced scientists' understanding of just how the Brassica family, which includes broccoli, cabbage, cauliflower, kale and Brussels sprouts, works in preventing cancer. When these vegetables are cut, chewed or digested, a sulfur-containing compound called sinigrin is brought into contact with the enzyme myrosinase, resulting in the release of glucose and breakdown products, including highly reactive compounds called isothiocyanates.

These are potent inducers of the liver's Phase II enzymes, whose job is to detoxify carcinogens. In addition, research recently conducted at the Institute for Food Research in the U.K. shows that the compound, allyl isothicyanate, inhibits mitosis (cell division) and stimulates apoptosis (programmed cell death) in human tumor cells.[25]

Got all that? Good. If not, just remember this: Eat your broccoli!

Ready for the Kitchen: Broccoli is ready to harvest 65–70 days after planting transplants. Harvest when the main head is three to six inches in diameter and the flower buds are still tightly closed. Cut the main stem about six inches below the top of the head. Some varieties produce many secondary florets in the axils of the stems after the main head has been harvested. Store in perforated or open plastic bags for up to two to three weeks in the refrigerator. Freeze surplus.

Annual Savings: Approximately $45 per year per person on average.

14

Bugged!
What To Do When the
Extraterrestrials Attack

I can't think of a more painful experience in the life of a container gardener than waking up one morning to find holes in the leaves of a tomato plant. Or big, brown spots clinging to those prized hot peppers. Or curled leaves on the cucumber plants. It's the end of a long, hard trail.

Or is it?

Actually, container gardeners are fortunate that horticultural science has advanced to a stage where there's nearly a hundred-percent chance for complete recovery of plants fouled by even the most insidious of insects.

Nothing for you to worry about, you say? You run a clean ship? You've never had insect problems in your life? Well, don't be too confident, because sooner or later, you're going to have problems. I guarantee it.

We have to accept that fact because insects are everywhere. Unless you live in a bubble, they're in your home right now. You might not see them, but they're there. It's inevitable that, eventually, they're going to come in contact with your plants.

Oh, sure, growing plants in containers allows you to control a plant's environment more closely than if it were outside heeled into the ground — especially if that container is kept indoors. Certainly growing container plants indoors is a giant step forward toward eliminating contact with most of the usual bad guys that outdoor gardeners face. But it's not guaranteed that you're never going to have a problem.

That's because microscopic eggs — and sometimes even the insects themselves — are airborne. Each time you open a door or a window, you are exposing your plants to a variety of potential dangers. Sometimes the plant's natural mechanisms will successfully fight off attacking pests. Other times, not.

Fortunately, there are only a few common *indoor* insect pests: ants (rare), aphids (rare), mites, whiteflies, mealy bugs, leaf hoppers (rare) and scales. Specific insecticides (particularly environmentally safe biological products) work wonders in eliminating them without causing damage to the plants or the environment. If you object to the use of *any* chemical warfare, you can do what one plant shop owner in Chicago does:

"My *Schefflera* used to be plagued with mealy bugs, scale and spider mites, but I hated to use insecticides, particularly indoors. Then I developed the idea of wiping the leaves with a mild solution of Ivory Liquid and water (never use a harsh detergent, which could prove toxic to the plants). After I sponge both sides of each leaf, I place the plants in the bathtub and let the shower water rinse them clean. This also provides proper, thorough watering for the plants every three or four weeks, as necessary. Ever since I began this program, I haven't seen an insect within twenty feet of my plants...."

My own evaluation of this rather unusual approach to controlling insect attacks is that it's just that: control, not eradication. A giant *Schefflera* of mine was attacked once by spider mites. I battled them similarly, bathing each leaf and all of the stalks in a solution of Ivory Liquid and water. Then I tried another recommended solution: rubbing alcohol (extremely diluted) and water.

After each washing, I rinsed the plant thoroughly. The only improvement I saw was that the mites seemed to be cleaner.

Finally, I went to a chemical systemic followed by a potent inorganic spray. The results? I got rid of the spider mites. Just days before the *Schefflera* went belly up.

I don't mean to sound overly pessimistic — only realistic. I believe I could have gotten rid of the spider mites and saved the *Schef* had I taken a more sensible approach sooner. I believe, too, that the shop owner's approach to keeping insects from her *Schefflera* is a good one, if it's practiced before serious infestation occurs. Once the bugs have struck in full force, though, you'll have to strike back hard and fast.

Common Invaders

Let's take a look at some of the insect pests that are most likely to show up as uninvited guests on your container plants.

Ants aren't going to be much of a problem unless your home happens to be overrun with them or if you bring them in from outdoors in the dirt balls or pots of other specimens or if they have infested nursery-bought plants or shrubs that you bring directly into your home (never a good idea, by the way — always keep new plants destined for indoors outside or at least segregated until you have an opportunity to inspect them closely).

Ants don't damage plants directly, but they can transfer various diseases from a sick plant to a healthy one. They have the peculiar habit of picking up tiny hitchhikers called aphids and moving them from place to place on host plants. They encourage the aphids to chow down, after which the bugs emit a sweet "honeydew" that the ants carry back with them to their nests. The nectar often harbors a fungus called "sooty mold," which is transmitted from one plant to another as the aphids make their rounds.

When ants are a problem, I recommend a commercial ant trap: a small, enclosed tin with several holes punched in the side, containing food coated with slow-acting poison. When the ants carry the food back to their colony for the queen and others to feed on — poof! Give the ants a little extra incentive by sprinkling a few grains of sugar inside the holes in the trap.

If the ants don't seem to be affected by the trap at first, have patience. They often go through periods when they don't feed. Keep the traps around, and sooner or later they'll do the job.

Aphids attack all parts of a plant and suck the juices from it. Whole herds of these plant lice can be eradicated by hand, sprayed off by a strong stream of water or treated with insecticidal soap. For a stronger cure, you could use a product such as maliathon, although it is nasty stuff and not recommended, especially for food crops.

Aphids are extremely mobile. They crawl, of course, and some species fly. That means they'll move from one plant to another in a hurry if you don't take steps to isolate the infected specimens. In dry, warm weather, they reproduce very quickly, reaching staggering numbers within a week. The young mature in two weeks, and many are parthenogenetic (able to produce living young without fertilization); so, it's easy to see how large populations can build up in no time.

To control aphids, use insecticidal soap to strip them of their protective wax coating, dehydrating them. Mix 1 tablespoon of soap to 1 gallon of water, and spray. You can also kill aphids and other soft-bodied pests with garlic oil spray. Or dust your plants with diatomaceous earth (DE), which is lethal to aphids. Wear a mask when using DE, however, because the dust can easily go airborne.

Leaf hoppers are sometimes a problem with plants brought in from outside or from a nursery. These pests tend to cling to the bottom of leaves and eat small holes through to the top. More damaging than that, they occasionally transmit viral diseases from sick to healthy plants. Also, mature adults lay eggs among a small spray of white bubbles that looks something like foaming saliva. If you notice either adults or eggs, spray with insecticidal soap.

Mealy bugs are slow-moving, insidious pests covered with a mealy wax. They look like small dabs of white cotton. They, like aphids, are sucking insects. They can be eradicated in small numbers by dipping a Q-Tip in alcohol and dabbing each insect lightly. They may also be killed off by using insecticidal soap or DE.

Spider mites are tiny, eight-legged creatures barely visible to the unaided eye. They are appropriately named because they spin tiny webs in the axils of various fleshy-leaved plants — often your first indication of their presence. They can become serious pests: they have a short life cycle and a rapid rate of reproduction. Under favorable conditions large populations can build up quickly and suck the life from an otherwise healthy plant. Control with insecticidal soap.

Whiteflies are easily recognized, as a rule, as small, whiteflies (thus the name — clever, no?) on the underside of leaves. They are not true flies but rather relatives of mealy bugs, scales and aphids. They frequently fly away when disturbed, only to return all too quickly. As with aphids, whiteflies produce honeydew, which encourages sooty mold growth.

They will suck the life out of otherwise healthy plants. Fortunately, they can be controlled fairly easily by spraying with insecticidal soap. They can also be discouraged by the presence of African and French marigolds, which give off an aroma that is unpleasant to the insect.

Scales are among the most objectionable of insects. They resemble small, brown barnacles and attach themselves to the underside of leaves and to main stalks and shoots. These pests can best be controlled by spraying with insecticidal soap or by dabbing with an alcohol-saturated Q-Tip.

These are the insect pests that are likely to enter your home and attack healthy plants. If you're a collector who digs up and transplants your own fruit trees and shrubs, you run a chance of bringing still other insects in with you. To be on the safe side, carefully check all foliage, branches and stems, preferably with a good, strong magnifying glass. (I'm betting Sherlock Holmes would have made an excellent horticulturist). If you bring in bare-root plants, check the root systems for insects and, in any event, rinse the roots in a mild solution of salt and water before rinsing clean.

If you bring in a collected plant with a ball of earth around the roots, pot the plant as soon as possible and saturate the surface of the soil with insecticidal soap to catch any emerging insects. After that, maintain the plant in isolation for several weeks and watch for signs of trouble.

Ladies in the Parlor

As most outdoor organic gardeners can tell you, ladybugs are terrific. These attractive little beetles have voracious appetites: they eat up to two hundred aphids (their preferred cuisine) a day. When aphids aren't present, they'll graciously substitute spider mites, white-fly eggs and even mealy bugs. So what does all this have to do with you if you're an indoor gardener?

If destructive insects are a real problem in your home, give some

One of the best friends a gardener has, the common ladybug consumes thousands of aphids a month.

careful, unprejudiced thought to releasing from fifty to a hundred lady-bugs among your plants. Install a plant light above infested trees and shrubs, if there's not one there already, and keep it going from dawn until dark. The light will attract the ladybugs and tend to keep them from wandering all over the house. The little beetles will stick around, gorging themselves on whatever bugs come to mandible, until their meal tickets have all expired. Then they will meet a similar fate (or, if you're a softy, you can try collecting them in a small net and releasing them to eat again outdoors).

Considering that ladybugs are so inexpensive, easy to maintain (just store them dormant in the refrigerator until time for release), undemanding and effective, you can hardly choose a better insect fighter, indoors or out. (Of course, they can't be trained to "fetch," so don't get rid of Fido.) Ladybugs are available by mail, over the Internet and locally from numerous sources.

Praying for Help

Another outdoor predator that has been used beneficially indoors is the praying mantis, named for the unique position in which it holds its two front, uhh, hands. Although perfectly harmless to humans and pets, they have sharp jaws that do a quick and effective job of controlling insect pests such as aphids, mealy bugs and others.

As with ladybugs, once the mantises have exhausted their food supply, they should be transferred outdoors — they can easily be picked up and carried outside — to continue their handiwork there.

Better Living through Chemistry?

There are many types of insecticides on the market, some of which have been around for decades. Some are relatively benign. Others can be deadly.

Before World War II, we knew precious little about chemical warfare. Afterwards, we knew plenty. As a result, an explosion of pest-control research that began in the 1940s provided a steady stream of data and many new compounds effective against an army of destructive insects. Lead arsenate, Paris Green and hellebore had once been the most commonly used garden insecticides, but postwar gardeners quickly discovered that the chlorinated hydrocarbons (such as DDT, chlordane and dieldrin), along with the organic phosphates, work more quickly and effectively. Over the next 30 years, these and similar compounds were widely used and equally widely abused.

As Rachel Carson, author of *A Silent Spring,* and a whole host of newly emerging environmental scientists burst onto the scene, we came to understand that many

Known for attacking more than corn, the corn borer has a voracious appetite and a reputation for wreaking havoc in gardens.

chemical insecticides were doing more harm than good. Some have since been banned for use in the United States and Canada, although they are still widely used throughout much of the rest of the world.

Regardless of their potential harm, sooner or later you're going to find yourself faced with the question: Do I use inorganic insecticides or not?

Before answering that question, remember that all chemical compilations (including commonly available plant food and fertilizers, by the way) can be hazardous to your health, as well as to the environment. So, the first thing to know about using inorganic pesticides is *don't.* Or, at least, don't without extreme caution.

If you must use a nychemical compound, never go overboard. Always read all labels carefully before opening a can or bottle. Follow directions precisely. Wear gloves and eye protection. Choose insecticides targeted to specific hosts as opposed to wide-spectrum or multi-purpose pesticides. And remember, if a little is good, a lot could be deadly.

Organic or Synthetic?

I consider myself an organic gardener. I mulch my outdoor vegetable garden and wouldn't come within fifty feet of it with an inorganic pesticide. But, outdoors, I don't have to. When insects strike, as they do every year, there are always natural checks around to draw upon. There are ladybugs, lacewings and praying mantises to release into the garden. There are birds that are attracted to nature's bountiful harvest of pests. There are harmless powders (such as finely screened lime and everyday kitchen flour) to sprinkle over vines to keep away cucumber beetles. There are pest-repellent flowers to plant and traps to set.

Together, these stratagems work well enough to assure that I'm left with a majority of the crop by the end of the season. And that's good enough for me.

Indoor gardening is another matter. We don't have the vast array of pest-fighters available to us that Mother Nature has at her disposal. Still, I try to use organic insect control wherever possible.

The best organic, non-polluting, non-hazardous pest fighter I've found is everyday insecticidal soap. That's a widely used phrase for any non-detergent soap not containing phosphates and other potentially harmful ingredients. One such soap available at most health-food stores is Ecover's Ecological Laundry Wash. It's made from plant-based soap, plant-based surfactants, water, citric acid (Vitamin C), citrate and vegetable ethanol. Another is Castile soap. Not only are these soaps non-polluting but also they work wonders on everything from house flies and roaches to ants and mealy bugs.

There are other organic pesticides equally effective and relatively harmless to the environment. Research into new compounds and techniques grows daily, exploding into some very unlikely areas. For example, some organic diseases can be used to eradicate harmful insects. The spores of a certain insect-attacking bacteria have been concentrated and used to control Japanese beetle grubs. The bacteria (*Bacillus popilliae*) give the grubs a fatal disorder called milky spore disease.

D.J. Herda

Tomato cutworms rarely destroy a tomato crop, but one worm can do some serious damage to a plant overnight— and they rarely travel in packs of one!

Another organic insecticide attacks leaf-eating caterpillars of the order *Lepidoptera*, which includes the tomato hornworm, the cabbage looper, the inchworm, the "bagworm," the tent caterpillar and many others. This insecticide, called *Bacillus thuringiensis*, is non-polluting and widely available in several commercial products.

Another avenue of research into pest control involves sterilizing insects so that they are unable to reproduce in quantities large enough to do serious damage. Some kinds of insects have been sterilized by radiation, and others have had their reproductive capacity knocked out chemically.

While sterilization by radiation is not particularly practical for the average home gardener, it illustrates the wide range of practices employable in stopping destructive insects dead in their tracks.

But just as you shouldn't try to kill an elephant with a fly swatter, you shouldn't use a Sherman tank to smash an ant. The key to successful and effective use of any insecticide is to match the method to the job.

The insecticides I've mentioned are only a few of the ones available to indoor gardeners. Others include microbial insecticides, botanical insecticides, chlorinated hydrocarbons, organic phosphates, systemics, carbamates, oil sprays, miticides and poison baits. For various reasons, some are less suitable for indoor use than others. Those that I recommend when called for follow.

Microbial Insecticides

Both milky spore disease (*B. Popilliae*) and *B. thuringiensis* are excellent means of fighting off insect attack, but they work only for specific insects. Milky spore disease attacks only the grubs of Japanese beetles and of similar, closely related insects. The spores cause the grubs' body fluid to turn a milky white color, after which the grubs die. Although the spores are usually applied to lawns, where they work their way into the ground and are ingested along with roots eaten by the beetle grubs, they can also be useful to container gardeners. If you grow container plants outdoors, you may be able to protect some of your prized possessions from attacks by beetles by applying the spores to your lawn, where the grubs reproduce.

B. thuringiensis has been proven effective against more than a hundred different species of *lepidopterus* larvae. As with milky spore disease, you may utilize the bacteria where larvae could cause problems with outdoor container plants. *B. thuringiensis* works after larvae eat the spores with the dusted or sprayed foliage. The pests die from intestinal paralysis within 48 hours.

Best of all, both milky spore disease and *B. thuringiensis* are safe for humans, wildlife, fish and beneficial insect parasites and predators.

Botanical Insecticides

As the name implies, these are insecticides obtained from crushed or powdered parts of plants, or botanicals. They're safe for humans and most wildlife. This group includes nicotine for fighting aphids and various other sucking insects; pyrethrum, for sucking insects and flies; rotenone, a general insecticide (it's harmful to fish, so avoid use near ponds and aquariums); and sabadilla, a general insecticide with less killing power than rotenone.

Organic Phosphates

This group of insecticides kills by disabling the nervous system. Some of the products in this group should *not* be used indoors. They may be used very cautiously outdoors, on the porch or in the garage. Be especially careful to read the labels on these products before purchase and use. Malathion, the most widely used of the organic phosphates, kills scales, whiteflies, mealy bugs and other insects. Diazinon, which is marketed under the name Spectracide, is a general, broad-range insecticide. TEPP, for aphids, mites and other sucking insects, is highly toxic to humans, but its toxicity breaks down quickly.

Systemics

These chemicals are absorbed through the roots of plants and distributed throughout the plants' systems. Sucking insects and mites that feed on the treated plants are then poisoned. Although not recommended for food crops for obvious reasons, systemics (especially the powders and granules) are a generally safe, effective means of dealing with sucking pests on non-food plants. Do not use where dirt-eating pets or young children are present! Included in this group of insecticides are Bidrin, demeton (under the name Systox), phosdrin and phorate (under the name Thimet).

Miticides

As the name implies, these insecticides are formulated expressly for control of mites. Perhaps the most widely used miticide indoors is dicofol (under the name Kelthane). Others include ovex (under the name Ovotran), Aramite and Dimite. The last two should *not* be used on food crops.

Dormant Oil Sprays

This group includes various emulsified oils for the control of scale insects, mealy bugs and the eggs of many insects and mites. The sprays are used on dormant trees. Oil sprays may injure thin-barked trees, so I recommend that you use them rarely and with extreme caution. A good example is oil dormant (also known as Superior Oil).

Summer Oil Sprays

These insecticides, which are used on certain trees during their growing period, have characteristics similar to those of dormant oil sprays. A good example is oil summer (under the name Superior Oil). It is especially effective for fighting mites and scale on citrus trees.

I mention all of these different insecticide types because I believe you should be aware of their existence and know a little bit about how they do their jobs. I do not talk about them because I suggest you rely upon them for simply insect eradication around your container plants — at least not until you have exhausted all other avenues of control.

Often, the simplest solution to a problem is the best. When it comes to controlling insects, physically removing them from the infested plant, either by plucking them off with your fingers or by washing them off with a strong spray from the garden hose, will do the trick.

If that approach is impractical, there's always the old standby of insecticidal soap. A light misting repeated on a daily basis for up to a week should kill off any delayed hatches of the little beasts. I have used it successfully against virtually every insect I have come across, all without fear of harmful effects on the environment.

Give it a try.

01:00   IN A MINUTE

- If you're a container gardener—indoors or out—accept the fact that, sooner or later, you're going to have to deal with insects.

- While numerous insecticides are available, you should use only those that are safe for food crops and around people, pets and the environment.

- Use natural predators as a means of controlling insect infestations wherever possible, even inside the home.

- When washing down your infested plants doesn't do the trick, try spraying with a mixture of water and insecticidal soap.

Dwarf Blueberry (*Vaccinium uliginosum*)

Habit: Shrub

Cultivars: Several cultivars have been developed specifically for use in containers. The most compact and most prolific bearers are:
- Tophat and Northsky

Blueberry

Recipes for Success

Seed or Transplants: Transplants

Pot Size: Medium to large

Water: Water container thoroughly, allowing the soil to dry out between waterings. Too much moisture can lead to fungal diseases.

Comments: Dwarf blueberries are a great choice for container growing. These grow to only 1½ feet in height. The plants feature an attractive compact mounded shape which is loaded with white blossoms in the spring and red foliage in the fall. In late August, plants yield hundreds of full-size, firm, flavorful blue fruit with wild blueberry flavor. Growing blueberries presents a challenge to in-ground gardeners because the plants require soils that are acid, well-drained, loose and high in organic matter—a rare find in most parts of the country. That makes growing blueberries in containers especially attractive. As a bonus, the plants are self-pollinating, meaning they will set fruit indoors without the aid of wind or insect pollinators.

Seeds: N/A

Transplants: Place in hole no deeper than original root ball and tamp around stem firmly with hands.

Soil: Blueberries require a lower (more acidic) soil pH than do most other fruit shrubs and trees, a maximum of 5.0–5.3 or lower. Supply regularly with an acidic fertilizer as prescribed, since blueberries are heavy feeders. Keep soil loose and loamy.

Insects: The primary insect problems are cranberry fruitworm (which ties berry clusters together with silk), Japanese beetles and the Oberea stem borer. **Solutions:** Spray with biologically friendly non-detergent soap mixed with water (1T per gallon water). Pick off and dispose of larger insects.

Diseases: Blueberries may be troubled by fungal leaf spots, fruit rots, root rot and gray mold. **Solutions:** Spray with appropriate biologically safe fungicide. (See Chapter 15.) Avoid excessively wet soil and prolonged exposure to cool temperatures, conditions favorable to fungal disease.

Mike Hillis

Dwarf Blueberry (*Vaccinium uliginosum*)

Health Benefits: By now, nearly everyone has heard about the health-giving properties of blueberries. I'm here to tell you that it's not true. Everything that has been said has been understated. For example:

Of 60 fruits and vegetables tested at Tufts University for their antioxidant capability, blueberries came in first. They have the highest rating for their ability to destroy damaging free radicals. Rich with antioxidant phytonutrients called *anthocyanidins*, blueberries neutralize free radical damage to the collagen matrix of cells and tissues that can lead to cataracts, glaucoma, varicose veins, hemorrhoids, peptic ulcers, heart disease and cancer. Anthocyanins, the blue-red pigments found in blueberries, strengthen the veins and vascular system and enhance the effects of vitamin C to increase capillary action and stabilize the collagen matrix (the ground-zero substance of all body tissues).

While red wine is renowned for being a great source of antioxidant anthocyanins, blueberries provide a third more of these free radical fighters. And the beneficial effects of blueberries on the eyes are not difficult to see. Extracts of bilberry (a cousin of blueberry) have been shown in numerous studies to improve night vision. As a bonus, eating three or more servings of the fruit per day may lower your risk of age-related macular degeneration (ARMD), the primary cause of vision loss in older adults, by 36 percent, compared to persons who consume less than 1½ servings of fruit daily.

If you think blueberries are terrific, you must be eating blueberries, as numerous tests have shown that this remarkable fruit can help protect the brain from oxidative stress and may reduce the effects of age-related diseases such as Alzheimer's and dementia. Studies have shown that diets high in blueberries improved both the learning capacity and motor skills of aging animals dramatically, making them mentally equivalent to much younger ones.

Add to all of this the fact that blueberries promote gastrointestinal health, protect against ovarian cancer and generate greater waste elimination, and you begin to get the overall picture:

Blueberries. There's no single healthier fruit known to mankind.

Ready for the Kitchen: Many blueberries exhibit the best quality when picked every five to seven days, depending on temperature. Keep birds from beating you to the harvest by covering shrubs with bird netting as berries begin to ripen. Dwarf blueberries yield full-sized fruit, ranging in quantity from 2–5 pounds per bush or more once mature, usually 60–90 days after flowering.

Annual Savings: Approximately $68 per year per person on average.

15

Fungus Among Us:
Wilt Thou No More

Unlike most insect attacks, diseases that are primarily fungal or bacterial in nature are impossible to see coming and more difficult to diagnose. It's true that no two scabs, wilts or rots look exactly alike, but many are so similar to the untrained eye that more than a little guesswork is involved in identifying the culprit for treatment.

Luckily, there are some broad-spectrum disease treatments on the market that require less precise identification. I don't normally like to use such products on my plants because they tend to "over-medicate" the patient; but sometimes they are the best (if not the only) alternative to losing a plant (or at least the season's harvest) to disease.

But commercial fungicides are only the tip of the iceberg when it comes to treating plants for disease. Over the years, science and — many times — observant and creative home gardeners have come up with various preventative measures, as well as a few pretty safe all-around cures on their own. Here are a few of the better ones.

Apple Cider Vinegar Fungicide
Leaf spot
Mildew
Scab
Mix 3 tablespoons of cider vinegar (standard 5% acidity) with one gallon water and spray in early morning on infested plants. Good treatment for black spot on roses and aspen trees, as well as on fruits and vegetables.

Baking Soda Spray Fungicide
Anthracnose
Early tomato blight
Leaf blight
Leaf spot
Powdery mildew
General fungicide

Sodium bicarbonate, more commonly known as baking soda, possesses fungicidal properties. Use after hosing down plants infected with powdery mildew. Use at first sign of the disease.

Mix 1 tablespoon baking soda, 2½ tablespoons vegetable oil and 1 gallon of water. Shake thoroughly to form a suspension. Add ½ teaspoon of pure Castile soap, and spray on infected plants. Be sure to agitate the sprayer from time to time to keep mixture in suspension. Saturate both upper and lower leaf surfaces and spray some on the soil. Repeat every five to seven days as needed.

Chive Spray Fungicide
Apple scab
Downy mildew

Place a handful of chopped chives in a heatproof glass or stainless steel container and cover with boiling water. Let this sit until cool. Strain and spray on plants two or three times a week.

Manure Tea Antibacterial
Blight
It is also a general antibacterial.

Fill a 30-gallon trash can with water. Let sit for 24 hours to evaporate any chemical additives (or use collected rain water). Add about four shovels of manure and cover. Let it sit for two to three weeks, stirring once a day. Strain and spray on soil and foliage as required. Avoid using on seedlings, which may develop damping-off disease. Note: Various manure teas supply varying nutrients as follows:

- Chicken manure: rich in nitrogen, used for heavy feeders such as corn, tomatoes and squash
- Cow manure: high in potash, used for root crops
- Rabbit manure: promotes strong leaves and stems
- Horse manure: used for healthy leaf development

Compost Tea Antibacterial/Fungicide
General antibacterial/fungicide
If you're a gardener and you're not composting your vegetative wastes (grass clippings, leaves, vegetable trimmings, watermelon rind, etc.), you're missing out on a great source of free and invaluable plant food and natural pesticide.

Make and use just the same as you would the manure tea, except without animal wastes.

Corn and Garlic Spray Fungicide/Preventative
General fungicide/preventative
Gather a handful of corn leaves, clematis leaves (any kind) and as much of the papery outer leaves of garlic as you can. Process in a blender until smooth. Mix with sufficient water to make a thin liquid. Let sit for an hour, strain and spray on plants as a preventative.

Couch Grass Rhizome Tea Fungicide
Mildew
It is also a general fungicide.
Put a handful of fresh rhizomes in a glass or stainless steel container. Pour 1 quart of boiling water over rhizomes, cover and allow to steep for 10 minutes. Strain, let cool and use at once.

Elder Leaf Spray Fungicide
Black spot
Mildew
Simmer 8 ounces of leaves in 16 ounces of water for 30 minutes. Stir the mixture thoroughly and strain. Mix 16 ounces of warm water and 1 tablespoon of Castile soap. Add soap mixture to the elder water, and spray as required. Note: Set your sprayer to a coarse or large droplet setting to prevent mixture from clogging sprayer.

Garlic Fungicide 1
Leaf spot
Mildew
It is also a general fungicide.
Combine 3 ounces of minced garlic cloves with 1 ounce of mineral oil and allow to soak for 24 hours. Strain and set aside. Mix 1 teaspoon of

fish emulsion with 16 ounces of water and add 1 tablespoon of Castile soap. Slowly combine the fish emulsion water with the garlic oil. Store in sealed glass container in refrigerator for up to several months. To use, mix 2 tablespoons of garlic oil with 1 pint of water and spray.

Garlic Fungicide 2
General fungicide
Insect repellent
Blend 1 head of garlic with 3 cups water, 2 tablespoons canola oil (for a binder), 4 hot peppers and a whole lemon. Steep mixture overnight. Strain through fine strainer cheesecloth. Use at the rate of 4 tablespoons per gallon of water. Store unused portion in the refrigerator.

Horseradish Fungicide
General fungicide
Soil cleanser
Penn State University announced in 1995 that minced horseradish root holds promise in decontaminating wastewater. Other findings show that it may also help clean contaminated soils. The university's Center for Bioremediation and Detoxification reports that minced horseradish combined with hydrogen peroxide can completely remove chlorinated phenols and other contaminants found in industrial wastes. Experiments involve applying the mixture directly to contaminated soils or growing horseradish in contaminated soil and tilling the roots under immediately before applying hydrogen peroxide.

The cleansing properties of horseradish have been known for more than a decade, although creating a purified form has been far too expensive. This method has been proven to be equally effective for home garden use at a fraction of the cost.

Horseradish Tea
Brown rot
It is also a general fungicide.
You can make a tea from horseradish roots to use as a preventative spray for fungal diseases, most notably brown rot in apple trees. The white flesh of the horseradish root also contains significant amounts of calcium, magnesium and vitamin C to help nourish the plant.

Process one cup of roots in food processor until finely chopped. Combine with 16 ounces of water in a glass container and allow to soak for 24 hours. Strain liquid, and discard the solids. Mix liquid with 2 quarts of water and spray.

Hydrogen Peroxide Antibacterial/Fungicide
General antibacterial/fungicide
Hydrogen peroxide prevents disease spores from adhering to the plant tissue without causing harm to plants or soil. Always test on a small portion of plant tissue first for any negative reactions; avoid using on tender seedlings.

Spray plants with undiluted 3% hydrogen peroxide weekly during dry weather and twice a week during wet weather. If you already have problems, this may be used as a direct treatment.

Milk for Mildew Fungicide
Mildew
It is also a general fungicide.
Use a 50/50 mixture of milk and water. Spray plants thoroughly every three or four days during infestation, or weekly as a preventative. Milk can also be mixed at a rate of 2 ounces milk to 18 ounces of water and used as a spray every seven to ten days to treat mosaic disease on cucumber, tomato, squash and lettuce.

Milk and Anti-Transpirant for Tomato Virus
Tomato virus
It is also a general antibacterial.
This anti-transpirant protects the plant surface against disease spores while the skim milk provides the tomato plant with calcium, which is commonly deficient in tomato plants. Anti-transpirants are harmless and will not block the pores of the plant tissue.

Mix ½ teaspoon of commercial anti-transpirant (Cloudcover, Wilt-pruf, etc.) with 8 ounces of skim milk and 1 gallon of water. Spray plants. Clean out sprayer when finished and flush with fresh water. Note: an equivalent of prepared powdered milk may be substituted for the skim milk. Also, removing lower leaves on the plant may help reduce likelihood of contracting disease spores from the ground.

Damping-Off Disease Fungicide
Damping-Off Disease
Always use a sterile growing medium such as mixes of vermiculite and
Perlite for your seed-starting medium, as these should not contain
the fungi that cause damping-off disease. Water seedlings with room-
temperature water. (Cold water stresses plants, making them more vulnerable to disease.)

1. Chamomile Spray
Besides providing a good night's sleep, chamomile tea used on seed-
starting mix will help prevent damping-off. A concentrated source of
calcium, potash and sulfur, it is an effective food and a potent fungus
fighter. May also be used as a seed soak prior to planting to reduce
chances of damping-off occurring.

Pour 2 cups boiling water over ¼ cup chamomile blossoms. Allow to
steep until cool and strain into a spray bottle. Use as needed. Refrigerate
for up to two weeks. Chamomile blossoms can be purchased at health
food stores and at grocery stores in the form of tea bags.

2. Seaweed Spray
Seaweed is rich in nutrients and everything that young seedlings require; it can also be used to prevent damping-off.

Make a mixture adding ⅔ cup of kelp concentrate to 1 gallon of water
and spray as required.

3. Horsetail Tea (Equisetum arvense)
The common horsetail plant, which is very invasive in the garden, is rich
in silicon and helps plants to resist fungal diseases by increasing their
light-absorbing capabilities. Use on peach trees to control peach leaf
curl. Use on most plants to combat powdery fungi and on vegetables
and roses to control mildew. Safe and effective for indoor use.

In a glass or stainless steel container, mix ⅛ cup dried horsetail in 1
gallon non-chlorinated water. Bring to a boil and simmer for ½ hr. Cool
and strain. Store concentrate in a glass container for up to one month.
Dilute mix, adding 5–10 parts of non-chlorinated water to one part concentrate. Spray plants that show any symptoms of fungal disease every
three or four days. Spray seed-starting mixture to prevent damping-off.

4. Sphagnum Moss

Commonly available at garden and nursery centers, sphagnum moss makes a good damping-off preventative while it helps retain moisture.

Spread finely milled sphagnum peat moss on the soil surface of your seed beds or flats to prevent damping-off.

5. Powdered Cinnamon

Everyday garden-variety (make that kitchen-variety) cinnamon is a safe, effective means of preventing damping-off.

Sprinkle powdered cinnamon on the surface of your sterile planting medium. Don't worry if you get cinnamon on your plants as it will not hurt even the most tender of seedlings. This preventative is nearly 100% effective in preventing damping-off.

Not all of these home-concocted remedies are guaranteed to work for *you*. But they have been time-tested and shown to work for others, including yours truly. As with treating any type of pest, the sooner you identify and target a problem for treatment, the greater your chances of success will be.

01:00   IN A MINUTE

- Fungal, viral and bacterial diseases can strike quickly and be very damaging to plants and produce if left untreated.

- A wide range of commercial products, including several broad-spectrum pesticides, are available for treatment, but always use these products with caution and generally as a last resort.

- Many natural remedies can be concocted at home and applied to affected plants more inexpensively and safely with impressive results

---

Dwarf Peach (*Prunus persica*)

Habit: Tree

Cultivars: Several varieties are available, including:
- Golden Glory and Bonanza

Seed or Transplants: Transplants

Pot Size: Large

Water: Water container thoroughly, allowing the soil to dry out between waterings. Too much moisture can lead to fungal diseases.

Dwarf Peach (*Prunus persica*)

Comments: Dwarf peach trees are very popular for use in container gardening. They produce fruit of the same size, color and quality as larger standard trees. Dwarf trees are developed through the use either of dwarfing rootstocks or genetic manipulation. Genetic dwarfs usually have very short internodes and dense foliage but have to be pruned, fertilized and cared for in the same manner as a standard tree.

Genetic dwarf fruit trees are compact and short; few exceed 7 feet in height, with an equal spread. Like all dwarf species, they bear normal-size fruit.

Sunlight is the key to maximizing fruit production. Pick an area where the trees will be in the sun most or all of the day. Early morning sun helps dry dew from the trees, reducing the incidence of fungal disease.

Seeds: N/A

Transplants: Place in hole no deeper than original root ball and tamp around stem firmly with your hands.

Soil: Although peach trees will grow well in a wide range of soil types, a deep soil ranging in texture from a sandy loam to a sandy clay loam is preferred. Peach trees are extremely sensitive to poorly drained soils. In areas of poor drainage, roots will die, resulting in stunted growth and eventual death of the tree. Most fruit trees, including peaches, grow best where the soil pH is at or around 6.5.

Insects: There are a number of insects that cause damage to peach flowers, fruit, limbs, twigs and trunks. Among the most destructive in home garden plantings are peach tree borers, plum curculio, scale, catfacing insects (stink bugs and tarnished plant bugs), oriental fruit moths, Japanese beetles and the green June beetle. **Solutions:** Spray with biologically friendly non-detergent soap mixed with water (1T per gallon water). Pick off and dispose of larger insects.

Diseases: The most damaging peach disease is a fruit rot commonly called brown rot. Other diseases of peaches include scab, Rhizopus rot, leaf curl, bacterial spot, peach phony, oak root rot and nematodes. **Solutions:** Spray with appropriate biologically friendly fungicide. (See above.) Avoid excessively wet soil and prolonged exposure to cool temperatures, conditions favorable to fungal disease.

Health Benefits: Peaches and nectarines provide good sources of carotenes, potassium, flavonoids and natural sugars. Both closely related fruits are good sources of lycopene and lutein. Lutein gives the red, orange and yellow colors to fruits and vegetables. These phytochemicals are especially beneficial in the prevention of heart disease, macular degeneration and cancer.

Ready for the Kitchen: Peaches are ready for harvest when they turn yellow and feel slightly giving to the touch, usually around the end of August. Pick by holding the fruit firmly and twisting it until it breaks free from the stem.

Annual Savings: Approximately $48 per year per person on average.

16

Harvest Time
and the Pickin' Is Easy

Wee Willie Keeler, one of the best hitting outfielders in the history of major league baseball, once summed up his success at the plate. "Hit 'em where they ain't."

Well, in the only slightly less popular sport of major league container gardening, we have a similar saying. "Pick 'em when they're ripe."

There might be times, I suppose, when you'll want to harvest something before it has had a chance to fully ripen, such as a green bell pepper, which is green only because it was picked before it had an opportunity to ripen into the red bell pepper so sought after and overpriced in stores.

By and large, though, we want to pick our produce at the absolute height of its fully ripened glory. Or, on second thought, make that ten minutes beforehand. It might take that long just to get it into the house.

Why the big rush to pick things ripe?

Think of the lifespan of a fruit or vegetable as you think of a clock, with 12:00 noon being the ripening hour. If we define ripeness as the peak of development according to taste, anything picked before noon will not yet have achieved its full mouth-watering potential, and anything picked after the bewitching hour will be on its way toward epicurean disaster.

How, though, do we know when that bewitching hour is? I mean, I'd hate to see you toil over that prized cucumber for three months only to pluck it from the vine 10 days after its peak.

Dwarf by Any Other Name

Miniature fruit trees were discovered as natural mutations of seed trees eons ago. While agriculturists searched for a naturally occurring dwarf peach tree, millions of trees were grown in test plots to find the tiny percentage of seedlings that had the sort of genetic mutation that resulted in compact growth characteristics. Once those seedlings were singled out, breeders such as Floyd Zaiger and Fred Anderson (whose work is now being carried on by Norman Bradford) hand pollinated the seedlings from varieties with the greatest quality.

After years of breeding to blend the genes of those progeny having good-tasting fruit and appealing color with those offering miniature size, the best trees went to trial plots scattered around the country for test growing and observation. The best from those trials were then propagated for retail sale.

In all, it took two decades to complete the first full cycle of breeding from a natural seedling mutation to a reliable source of miniature trees for sale at your local nursery.

There are several ways to estimate when to harvest your fruits and vegetables. You can get a very rough estimate based upon the guidelines on the seed packet, if you planted from seeds. You know: "60 days to harvest." But that is subject to a great deal of variance, depending upon growing conditions, seed condition when planted and other variables. Besides, that won't help you know when to harvest a tomato from a transplant you placed in a pot three weeks ago.

How do people determine the right harvest time, then? Mostly, they wing it. Experienced gardeners know from their past labors when a fruit or vegetable appears to be ready for harvest.

Here are a few tips to help you know what to pick, when to pick it — and how.

Apples: Often picked before they're ripe, apples that have an astringent, biting taste are not yet ready for harvest and will never become sweet or develop a good taste. Except for solid red varieties, apples are ready for picking when the basic green color shows considerable yellowing. The seeds should have turned fairly dark; if still green, the apples are not ready for harvest. Apples to be eaten soon should be allowed to ripen on the tree before picking, while those destined for storage can be picked a week or so before ripening. To harvest, lift an apple and twist it slightly; those that are ready should separate easily from the branch, and the stems should remain attached to the fruit.

Apricots: Pick when the color is deep yellow-orange and the fruit gives slightly under pressure from your fingers but is still firm. Often, that's two or three days after the birds discover their good fortune.

Asparagus: Cut or snap spears off at soil line when they average 6–10 inches in height and before the heads open. Stop harvesting when the average spear diameter is less than ¼ inch.

Beans (snap): Pick before you can see the seeds bulging inside the pods. They should snap easily in two. Check daily and pick in succession over the harvest season. It doesn't take long for beans to go from tender to tough, although if you do wait too long to harvest some beans, you can allow them to dry on the vine, shuck them and use them as dried beans in cooking.

Beets: These versatile roots are really a matter of personal preference when it comes to the right size for harvesting. They are ready any time after you see the beets shoulders protruding from the soil line. You can harvest and eat the green tops that you thin out of the rows.

Blueberries: Begin sampling fruit when it is large, round and deep blue to purplish in color. Not all berries will ripen at once, so you will need to harvest daily throughout the picking season.

Broccoli: Besides the main fruit, you can harvest and eat the unopened flower buds of broccoli. To remove the main head (ripe about the time flowers begin opening), cut with a sharp knife, leaving 4–6 inches of stem below the head.

Cabbage: The cabbage head will feel solid when gently squeezed . Cabbage needs to be harvested when it reaches maturity or it will continue to grow and split open.

Carrots: Carrots can be tricky to judge. The tops of the carrot will show at the soil line and you can gauge when the diameter looks right for your variety. If the diameter looks good (usually from ¾–1½ inches at the shoulder), chances are the length is fine too. But you will need to pull one to be certain. Carrots can be left in the ground once mature. A light frost is said to improve and sweeten the carrot's flavor.

Cherries: Use the taste test to determine degree of ripeness. Cherries should be sweet; dark cherries should be very dark in color.

Citrus: Lemons, limes, grapefruit and oranges that have matured to full size should be picked at the height of their color development, while still firm to the touch.

D.J. Herda

Knowing when to pick your fruits and vegetables in order to get the greatest taste and the most nutrients from your harvest makes container gardening all that much more rewarding.

Cucumber: Cucumbers race to the harvest with zucchini. Check daily and pick while young. Timing and length will vary with variety. The fruits should be firm and smooth. Over-ripe cucumbers can be very bitter or pithy, even before they start to turn yellow, so err on the side of an early harvest.

Eggplant: Slightly immature fruits taste best. The fruits should be firm and shiny. Cut rather than pull from the plant to avoid injury to the host.

Figs: These fruits should be allowed to remain on the tree until they are ripe. The flesh should be quite soft, and the proper color for the particular variety should be deep and fully developed. Figs will bend at the neck and hang limply on the branches as they get close to ripening. When picked, the stems should not exude any milky sap; if they do, they're not ripe enough for harvest. You may have to fight the birds for those last few days, however, as figs are a rare treat to many North American species.

Garlic: This one is a no-brainer. You know the garlic is ready for harvest when the tops fall over and begin to brown. It's like a neon sign: *Dig me now!* After that, dig — don't pull. Before storing, allow the bulbs to dry well to prevent them from rotting. Also brush the dirt off instead of washing.

Kale: Kale leaves can be plucked throughout the growing season. They should be a deep green with a firm, sturdy texture. Kale tastes best when harvested in cooler weather.

Kohlrabi: For the best texture, harvest once the fleshy swollen stem has reached 2–3 inches in diameter. Kohlrabi becomes tough and woody as it ages. Pull the plant or slice at the base to harvest.

Leeks: Harvest when they are about 1 inch in diameter.

Lettuce (head): Harvest once the head feels full and firm with a gentle squeeze. Hot weather will cause the plant to bolt, or go to seed, so grow when cool.

Lettuce (leaf): Harvest the entire plant in warm weather or only the outer leaves once the plant has reached about 4 inches in height, allowing the younger, inner leaves to grow.

Muskmelon (or cantaloupe): There are many varieties of muskmelon, but a general rule of thumb is that the color should change to beige and the fruit will "slip" from the vine when lifted. You should also be able to notice a sweet smell when ripe.

Nectarines: Pick when full size, colorful and slightly giving to the touch.

Onions (bulb): Dig once approximately half of the tops have ripened and fallen over and the bulbs are at least 2 inches in diameter. Wipe or rinse dirt off the bulbs and allow to dry in the sun.

Onions (bunching): Harvest before they become thicker than ½ inch in diameter.

Peaches: Peaches are ready for picking when most of the green ground color (the unripened color) has turned yellowish. The red color is not an indication of ripeness. For best quality, allow to ripen on the tree and eat shortly after harvest. Because peaches do not store well, enjoy fresh and freeze or preserve any extras.

Pears: Unusual in that pears ripen best off the tree, these fruits should be picked before fully ripe or the fruits will develop a grittiness and be subject to deterioration of the core. Harvest them while they are still good and firm and barely turning yellowish green, and allow them to ripen off the tree. Picking them too green may mean they will never get their best flavor. Winter pears, such as Anjou and Bosc, require at least 30 days of refrigeration after harvest in order to ripen properly.

The best way to tell when a pear is ready to pick is to squeeze it. If the fruit offers the slightest bit of "give," it's ready for picking. If it is rock-hard, it is not. When ripe, a pear should come away from the spurs easily when lifted and twisted slightly. Pears should be stored at about 32°F to prevent them from ripening. At room temperature, a pear will ripen and be ready to eat within three or four days.

Peas: The pea pods should look and feel full. Peas are sweeter if harvested before fully plumped. Use the taste test: they're ready for harvest when they taste sweet raw.

Peppers (bell or sweet): Harvest when fruit is full size and still firm of texture, whether picking green or red.

Peppers (hot): Harvest when fruit is full size, shiny green to red in color and firm of texture. To harvest for use dried, allow to turn red and dry on the plant.

Plums: With both Japanese and European varieties of plums, the taste test is the best way to determine harvest readiness. They should just be beginning to soften and be sweet and juicy on the tongue.

Potatoes: "New" potatoes can be harvested when the tops start to flower. Carefully dig at the outer edges of the row. For full-sized potatoes, wait until the tops of the potato plants dry out and turn brown. Begin digging from the outside perimeter and move cautiously toward the center of the patch in order to avoid slicing into potatoes. Be gentle!

Radishes: Radishes mature quickly. You will see the shoulders of the bulbs popping out of the soil line. If left too long, they will become tough and eventually go to seed. Harvest and use as soon as large enough.

Spinach: Spinach goes to seed quickly. Harvest by cutting at the soil line before you see a flower stalk beginning to shoot up.

Strawberries: Pick when fruit is fully formed and deep crimson in color. Not all berries will ripen at once, so you will need to harvest in succession throughout the picking season.

Tomatoes: Harvest tomatoes when they are pink to fully colored and slightly giving to the touch, but still firm. Gently twist and pull from the vine.

Turnips: The turnip shoulders should be about 2–2½ inches in diameter at the soil line when ready. Harvest once they reach maturity. Overripe turnips become woody.

Zucchini: Harvest when fruits are fully colored and still firm to the touch, 4 inches in length or longer.

A couple of additional points about harvesting are in order here. Sometimes, when a crop is particularly bountiful and we become satiated — with zucchini, for example — the extra produce can be dried, blanched and frozen, or canned and stored for future use. If you're not the Suzy Homemaker canner type, at the very least give away the excess to friends, neighbors and relatives. I guarantee they'll appreciate your thoughtfulness.

Also, whenever you're removing fruits and vegetables from the host plant, be careful to do so gently to avoid injuring the produce or the plant itself, where applicable. I keep a pair of sharp garden shears at the ready for just that task. That way, I spend less time tugging and yanking on recalcitrant produce that simply won't give up the ghost and more time preparing for a hearty meal.

Salud!

01:00   IN A MINUTE

- Knowing when fruits and vegetables are ready for harvest is an acquired skill that comes from years of experience.

- When harvesting produce, be careful not to injure the host plant.

- While some fruits and vegetables can be picked from the stalk, others should be clipped with a pair of sharp shears to avoid damaging the host plant.

Dwarf Nectarine (*Prunus persica*)

Habit: Tree

Cultivars: Several varieties are available, including:
- Sunglo, Redgold and Garden Delight

Seed or Transplants: Transplants

Pot Size: Large

Water: Water container thoroughly, allowing the soil to dry out between waterings. Too much moisture can lead to fungal diseases.

Comments: Dwarf nectarines are an easy way to provide your family with large, freestone, red-blushed fruit for up to a month. Ideal for small backyard planter beds and large containers, the plant offers a spring bonus of stunning pink blossoms that precede fruiting. Some dwarfs grow only to 6 feet tall, making them easy to care for and house. Garden Delight is self-fertile, with fruit ripening in August. Requires 500 hours of wintertime chilling to bear, so keep out of doors or in a cool place prior to spring leafing. Give full sun for best yields.

Dwarf Nectarine (*Prunus persica*)

Seeds: N/A

Transplants: Place in hole no deeper than original root ball and tamp around stem firmly with hands.

Soil: Although nectarine trees will grow well in a wide range of soil types, they prefer a deep soil ranging in texture from a sandy loam to a sandy clay loam. Nectarine trees are extremely sensitive to poorly drained soils. In areas of poor drainage, roots will die, resulting in stunted growth and eventual death of the tree. Most fruit trees, including peaches, grow best where the soil pH is near 6.5.

Insects: There are a number of insects that cause damage to nectarine flowers, fruit, limbs, twigs and trunks. Among the most destructive in home garden plantings are peach tree borers, plum curculio, scale, catfacing insects (stink bugs and tarnished plant bugs), oriental fruit moths, Japanese beetles and the green June beetle. **Solutions:** Spray with biologically friendly non-detergent soap mixed with water (1T per gallon water). Pick off and dispose of larger insects.

Diseases: The most damaging nectarine disease is a fruit rot commonly called brown rot. Other diseases of peaches include scab, Rhizopus rot, leaf curl, bacterial spot, peach phony, oak root rot and nematodes. **Solutions:** Spray with appropriate biologically friendly fungicide. (See Chapter 15.) Avoid excessively wet soil and prolonged exposure to cool temperatures, conditions favorable to fungal disease.

Health Benefits: Nectarines provide a plentiful, reliable sources of carotenes, potassium, flavonoids and natural sugars. They are a good source of both lycopene, with all of its cancer- and heart-preventative benefits, and lutein. Lutein gives the red, orange and yellow colors to fruits and vegetables. These phytochemicals are especially beneficial in the prevention of heart disease, macular degeneration and cancer.

Ready for the Kitchen: Nectarines are ready for harvest when they turn yellow, usually in early to late summer, and feel slightly giving to the touch. Pick by holding the fruit firmly and twisting it until it breaks free from the stem.

Annual Savings: Approximately $53 per year per person on average.

Who Cares?
Caring for Your Plants
When You're Away

So you have all your planters set up just the way you want them. The to-matoes are starting to ripen, the cucumbers are nearly ready to pick, the peppers are just beginning to turn red, the peas are filling out their pods and the figs are just about ready to pop.

And you get called out of town.

The family vacation to Disney World comes due — you know, that trip you've been salivating over taking with the wife and kids for nearly four months now.

Or there's an unexpected emergency or a wedding or a Bar Mitzvah or a death in the family in a city far away. And everyone has to go.

What do you do now?

Relax. You can always call a plant sitter. For ten bucks a day, she'll be glad to come over and water and mist and fertilize and talk to your prized possessions.

But do you trust a stranger to come into your home? And isn't ten dollars a day a lot to pay someone for merely plant sitting? It's not like she has to walk the dog. You don't even *have* a dog!

How about your neighbor? Can your neighbor stop by and water the plants a couple of times a week? Would that be enough? And would your neighbor be counted upon to do it right?

Of course, you could always pack up all your plants, load them into the back of the family 4 × 4 and motor them down to the local nursery where I'm sure they would take care of them for you — for fifty dollars a week or so. No guarantees of survival, of course. And you will have to *schlep* them back home upon your return.

Hey, this is beginning to look like a bit of a problem.

But wait a minute. Let's not panic. Let's think this whole thing through.

The first thing to ask yourself when the family has to bug out of the house and leave the plants to their own devices is this: For how long?

If you're looking at a couple of days away, no problem. Simply see to it that everything is well watered the morning you're scheduled to leave, and you should find a house full of healthy (if slightly thirsty) plants upon your return.

But if you're planning on shutting up the house for four days or longer, you're going to have to get creative. Your plants are going to need water, pure and simple. Here are a few suggestions as to how to get it to them, from the ridiculously costly to the sublime.

El Cheapo

The least expensive way to help your plants s-t-r-e-t-c-h out between waterings is also the simplest. Take some plastic wrap and stretch it across the tops of your planters. Fasten with rubber bands, bungee cords or masking tape, as required. Position the wrap as close to the plant's trunk or main stem as possible to avoid moisture from sneaking out there. The idea is that, as water evaporates from the potting mix, the excess will condense against the underside of the plastic wrap and, when it returns to its liquid state once again, fall back to the soil.

This is not a perpetual-motion machine, of course, since the plants, too, are drawing upon the moisture in the soil and releasing it in their transpiration process from the leaves back into the room. But airproofing the soil surface will extend the time required between waterings from, say, three to six days, which may be just enough time to get you through your business and back home again.

Cost: *nada.*

Another inexpensive means of helping your plants survive the coming drought is to move them all into the bathroom. Arrange them in the tub and turn on the shower — room temperature only, please! — to saturate them well.

Once that's done, close the stopper on the tub and fill with approximately ½ inch of water. Assuming the stopper doesn't leak, that should be more than enough water — as well as moisture from the evaporation into the surrounding air — to see the plants through until your return. If you have shower doors or curtains, closing them will help maintain a greenhouse effect.

Cost: *nada.*

El Cheapo Not Quite-o

If you find that you have more plants than bathtub space (and that could easily be the case), you may have to build a larger holding area from scratch. It's not as difficult as you might think.

For starters, locate a single place where you can congregate your plants. The corner of a basement would be fine, as well as a guest or utility room — anywhere you can squeeze them in together.

Next, construct a wooden frame out of 4" lumber large enough to contain the plants. It doesn't have to be fancy — four boards laid on end will work just fine.

Lay a 3-milimeter plastic tarp or drop cloth on the floor and over the frame, and fasten the plastic with staples or thumbtacks. Once you have created a water-tight enclosure, begin placing the plants inside the frame. Water the containers well, and add half an inch of water to your new "pond."

Voila!

Cost: About $25.

Expensive-o

If all that work is not your cup of tea, you can purchase a timer that attaches to your outside hose bibb and set it to go on as often as you wish — say, once a day at a certain hour for five minutes at a time. Attach quarter-inch tubing to the timer and run the tubing under the door sweep and into the house to your plants. (It makes matters simpler if you congregate all of your plants in a single room.) Place a dripper in line with the first container, and repeat the process until every pot in the house has been fitted with its own dripper. You can assure that the

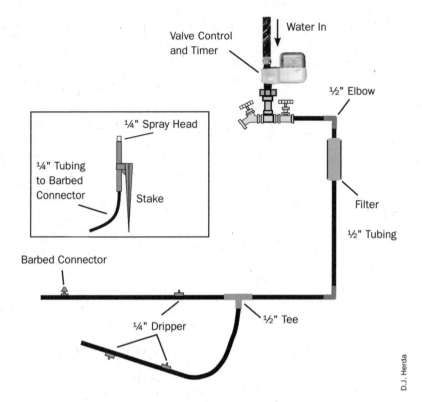

It can get to be rather convoluted, depending upon the number of plants you want to water and where they're located in and out of your home, but this quarter-inch system is my favorite for reliability and effectiveness.

dripper remains over the soil and doesn't slip off to one side by using a wire bail or wicket (similar to an oversized staple) to hold it in place.

Finally, turn on the water and test your new system. The timer should click to open at the specified time, sending a stream of water through the quarter-inch tubing and each of the drippers feeding the pots. It should click closed, ending the process, after the specified period of time.

This system — aside from looking a little strange to friends and family — should work just fine as long as you're away. When you return home, disconnect the hose and the drippers, and use the timer to regulate water to your outdoor plants.

Cost: About $40.

There are other commercial systems made specifically for watering indoor plants. One, by Claber, consists of a water reservoir and a battery-operated timer for handling up to 20 plants, according to the manufacturer. When the timer is triggered, the gravity-feed valve opens and the water runs out to the plants. It's low tech, but it works.

Cost: About $90.

There are other gravity-feed systems available, primarily drip-irrigation systems that water plants slowly and continuously. Although I haven't tried them all, they seem not to be the best options in the world, as they work on the principle of replacement: when the moisture in the soil becomes less dense than the moisture in the tube stuck into the soil, water from the reservoir is absorbed into the soil. This means that the soil never fully dries out, and that could create problems for long-term use.

01:00 IN A MINUTE

- Remember: When you leave home, you're going to have to make arrangements to care for your plants.

- If friends, neighbors and professional plant sitters aren't your cup of tea, you can always turn to mechanized plant-watering systems to do the job until your return home.

- In place of mechanical systems, with only a little bit of planning you can devise your own mini-greenhouse to see that your plants are never short of water and moisture.

Dwarf Apricot (*Prunus armeniaca*)

Habit: Tree

Cultivars: Several varieties are available, including:
- Stark Golden Glo, Garden Annie and Wilson's Delicious Dwarf

Seed or Transplants: Transplants

Pot Size: Large

Water: Water container thoroughly, allowing the soil to dry out well between waterings.

Comments: Of all the fruit trees, apricot is one of the most ornamental. The foliage—initially bronze when it opens, growing gradually darker green with maturity—is especially colorful. Unfortunately, most apricot trees bloom early, which makes them sensitive to late spring frosts. Several of the newer varieties, though, can tolerate more cold or bloom later in the season.

According to legend, George Washington boasted of apricot trees blooming in late March at Mt. Vernon.

To minimize frost damage, choose your apricot site carefully. Place outdoor pots on the tops or sides of hills or near lakes or ponds. Indoors, put them wherever you can give them plenty of light.

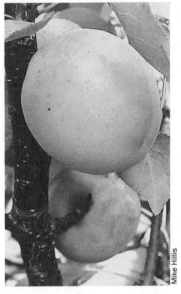

Dwarf Apricot (*Prunus armeniaca*)

Seeds: N/A

Transplants: Place in hole no deeper than original root ball and tamp around stem firmly.

Soil: Most soils are suitable for apricot provided the trees receive adequate water and fertilizer. The exception is heavy, poorly drained soils.

Insects: Insects and diseases are rarely a serious problem on apricots.

Diseases: Some of the problems you'll see with this tree are weather related. Brown rot, a fungus, can attack the plant during periods of high humidity and prolonged rainy spells. If temperatures go over 102°F just before the fruit matures, pit burn can develop.

Solutions: Treat with appropriate fungicide or horseradish tea. (See Chapter 15.)

Health Benefits: The nutrients in apricots are beneficial to the heart and eyes. The fiber works well to fight off various maladies. The high beta-carotene helps prevent the oxidation of LDL cholesterol, which in turn is useful in preventing heart disease. The flavor is useful in helping you to salivate.

Apricots contain vitamin A, which promotes good vision. Vitamin A is a powerful antioxidant that reduces free radical damage to the cells and tissues making up the eyes' lenses. This is important because the degenerative effects of free radicals may lead to cataracts or damage the blood supply to the eyes, resulting in macular degeneration. In a study of more than 50,000 registered nurses, researchers found that women who had the highest vitamin A intake had cataracts in 40 percent fewer cases than the control group.[26]

Apricots' high fiber content generates a wealth of benefits, including the prevention of constipation and digestive conditions such as diverticulosis. Most Americans ingest fewer than 10 grams of fiber per day. They could correct that deficiency by increasing the servings of fruit to three per day. That may sound like a lot, but it could be as simple a matter as tossing a banana into your morning smoothie, slicing some apricots over your cereal, topping off a cup of yogurt or green salad with a half cup of berries or snacking on an apricot or other fruit to reach your goal.

Ready for the Kitchen: Harvest apricots when they are fully colored and beginning to soften to the touch. Although harvest may include some succession, many varieties ripen within only a few days, so there is little window for delay once the fruits begin to ripen, usually in early summer.

Annual Savings: Approximately $71 per year per person on average.

18

Special Steps for
Fruiting Trees and Shrubs

There are no hard and fast rules for growing fruiting plants indoors successfully. As with any plants, indoors or out, some are easier to grow
than others. I've found that some tropical fruiting plants such as bananas
(*Musa*) and pineapples (*Ananas*) are easy to grow and induce into bearing fruit. Both of these plants are warm-climate plants that adapt well to
year-round indoor container growth.

Some people have told me that they have successfully brought various species of blueberry (*Vaccinium*) to fruit indoors in an acidic soil
of about 5.0 pH, but I myself have never grown them indoors. On the
other hand, one of the more trying fruiting trees I've grown in indoor
containers is the common apple (*Malus*). It's a hardy enough tree that
blooms profusely in its third year, and certainly there are enough species
and varieties to satisfy the indoor container grower. But turning blooms
into fruit is another story.

For one thing, apple trees, along with many blueberries and some
other flowering plants, are for the most part self-sterile. That means that
the pollen of one tree will not fertilize the pistils of the same tree. In
other words, to produce fruit, you need two to tango. They must have
cross-fertilization of two or more trees to succeed in fruiting. Thus, to
induce apple trees and other self-sterile trees to bear fruit indoors, you
must grow not one but at least two trees (and preferably more) in the
same general area.

Also, because apple trees (and most flowering trees and shrubs) normally require wind or insects such as moths, bees and wasps to complete pollination, the indoor gardener is at a lack and must take over the job himself.

With self-fertile plants, the pollen can be spread from flower to pistil simply by shaking the plant periodically while it is in bloom. With such self-sterile trees as apples, though, you must take a small brush and gently dust the blooms of one tree and then those of another, thereby transferring the pollen between the two plants.

This procedure requires more than a little time and patience each day that the plants are in bloom — and apples may have blooms for two or three weeks each spring!

Finally, the last and most trying aspect of bringing apple trees in particular to bear in containers indoors involves ambient temperature. In subtropical climates (and that includes your living room — sort of an artificial Hawaii where temperatures normally range from 68°F in winter to 90°F or more in non-air-conditioned homes in summer), apple trees set bloom but don't set fruit. Studies have shown that the winter temperatures must average below 48°F for four months out of the year if the apple tree is to complete its rest period, which is crucial to producing fruit.

Unless you're an Eskimo, that could be a problem indoors.

Beating the System

There are ways to beat the game, of course, if you're game enough yourself. If you have an unheated garage and live in a climate where winters are cold enough, you can move your apple trees there for wintering. Just make sure the thermometer in the garage doesn't drop *too* low, or the roots may freeze in the container.

And don't forget that out of sight does not mean out of mind. You'll still have to water the plants lightly on occasion even though they're dormant — perhaps as little as once a month. If the temperature plummets to freezing or lower, you should wrap the trees' containers in insulation to protect them against freezing solid. As the temperature begins to warm in March, you can gradually acclimate the plants to their summer surroundings and increase the amount and frequency of watering in keeping with their growth.

If you don't have a garage suitable for wintering your apple trees, perhaps your basement gets cold enough. Or, if worse comes to worst, you can move your trees outdoors and either sink the pots into the earth and cover them with a thick mulch of hay or move the pots to the patio, insulate them with roll insulation (available at most hardware stores and lumber yards) and entomb the pot and insulation in burlap.

Of course, these steps are necessary only if you're interested in producing fruit indoors. If you're satisfied with foliage and flowers and don't want the bother of fruit, don't worry about special wintering problems — any cool room will do.

If you're beginning to get the point that container apple trees should probably be left outdoors during the growing season, you're most likely right. Growing apple trees for fruit is much more difficult indoors than out.

Feed Follows Function

While everybody knows that nearly all potted plants require periodic feeding, most plants require more nutrients during their flowering period than at any other time of year. But they require the right nutrients in the right proportions to be beneficial.

Plants fed a food too high in nitrogen divert their efforts from producing flowers (and later, fruit) to producing additional foliage. To prevent that from happening, you should adjust the diet of your flowering trees and shrubs several weeks before flowering is expected.

Reduce the application of nitrogen and increase the availability of a phosphorous-rich food, which is necessary for the healthy production of flower buds.

There are, of course, many different fertilizers comprising a wide range of nutrient percentages available commercially. Throughout the growing season, I generally feed my foliage plants compost tea, consisting of water skimmed off the top of decomposing organic matter (the compost pile) which can contain carrot shavings, potato peels, ground apple cores, chopped orange skins, spent coffee grounds and whatever else I can find in the fruit-and-vegetable family! Occasionally, perhaps once every month or two, I subsidize this food with a full dose of commercial fertilizer or a handful of compost, something that provides my plants a strong dose of primary nutrients in the neighborhood of 15-30-15.

From one to two months before my flowering trees and shrubs are due to bloom, I curtail the use of compost tea and rely exclusively on the Miracle-Gro, along with a little bone meal (0-12-0). But, even though the directions on the package call for half a teaspoon of Miracle-Gro to two quarts of water applied every three or four weeks, I give my plants half that dosage, or one-fourth teaspoon to two quarts of water — applied twice as often, that is, every ten days to two weeks. The Miracle-Gro has twice as much phosphorous (30 percent) as nitrogen (15 percent); so the fertilizer encourages my plants to produce flowers at the expense of excessive foliar growth. I may also give them a healthy does of bone meal, which you may not want to do yourself if you have dogs around the house.

After the plants have finished flowering and setting fruit, I return to my original feeding schedule of compost tea and occasional applications of Miracle-Gro. Why Miracle-Gro when so many other products are on the market? For the best reason I know of — it works for me. I'm not saying something else wouldn't be just as efficient for you, and I'm not discouraging you from finding it. But, since I'm personally satisfied with the results of my feeding program, I'll stick to it.

However, sometime in the future I may try feeding my flowering plants a commercial food containing three times as much phosphorous as nitrogen — a 10-30-10 formula, for example. Experimentation, after all, is one of the joys of life — no less so with growing plants than with anything else.

Light and Water

Many people find that their flowering trees and shrubs produce plenty of blossom buds that fall to the ground before they open. Or the buds may open all right, but then shrivel up and fall off before pollination occurs. In these cases, chances are good that the cause is one of two culprits: insufficient light or insufficient water.

When a plant enters its flowering stage, it needs plenty of full-spectrum light — that is, light

D.J. Herda

Growing fruiting shrubs and trees indoors can present some special challenges, as with this dwarf nectarine, but it's worth all the extra fuss come harvest time!

containing all the rays present in the natural light of day. That includes ultraviolet rays.

Make sure your flowering plants receive from fourteen to sixteen hours of sunlight daily during their flowering season, or supplement the natural light with grow lights. These lights may be either fluorescent or incandescent. I like the fluorescents best, because they use less electricity than their incandescent counterparts, come in a wide variety of shapes and give off less heat. But incandescent bulbs have their merits, too. They are more widely available, cost less per bulb (although more per hour to operate) and may be used in almost any standard incandescent socket. (However, some incandescent bulbs — especially those of high wattage — produce so much heat that they should only be used in porcelain or insulated sockets.)

That other bogeyman, insufficient water, can be equally damaging to flowering plants. I know that I've been preaching to go easy on watering plants for most of my life. (It's the biggest single reason behind container garden failure.) And that's a sermon I'm going to stick with.

But during flowering season, even those trees and shrubs that normally prefer to dry out between watering (a category that includes nearly *all* plants) should be kept moist — not saturated, but damp.

Just how moist is moist is a question you yourself will have to answer. It's not as tough a task as it sounds, once you've gained a little experience. Generally, when a plant is in flower and the soil touch test tells you the plant would normally need watering in another couple of days, it's time to water. Some plants make the decision a little easier by turning their leaves down slightly as the soil begins to dry out. With careful observation, you may be able to "read" exactly when your plants want more water. Just remember that both flowers and fruit sap the plant of life-sustaining moisture far more quickly than foliar growth does; so keep a watchful eye on the soil.

01:00 IN A MINUTE

- Fruit plants need food, just as every plant does, but they need the right nutrients at the right time to produce those bumper crops you're looking for.

- Fruiting trees and shrubs require more water and light at the flowering and fruit-setting stage than at any other time.

Dwarf Banana (*Musa*)

Habit: Tree

Cultivars: Several varieties are available, including:
- Gran Nain, High Color Mini, Novak and Dwarf Cavendish

Seed or Transplants: Transplants

Pot Size: Large to extra large

Water: Water container thoroughly, and keep soil moist but not saturated throughout growing season; cut back on water during winter dormancy.

Comments: Banana is a tropical herbaceous plant consisting of an underground corm and a trunk (pseudostem) comprised of concentric layers of leaf sheaths. At 10 to 15 months after the emergence of a new plant, its true stem rapidly grows up through the center and emerges as a terminal inflorescence that bears fruit.

The flowers appear in groups (hands) along the stem and are covered by purplish bracts that roll back and shed as the fruit stem develops. The first hands to appear contain female flowers, which will develop into bananas (usually seedless in edible types). The number of hands of female flowers varies from a few to more than 10, after which numerous hands of sterile flowers appear and shed in succession, followed by numerous hands of male flowers, which also shed. Generally, a bract rolls up and sheds to expose a new hand of flowers almost daily.

Because banana trees are rapid growers, they require a balanced fertilizer once a month. Use an 8-10-8 for best results.

Seeds: N/A

Transplants: Place in hole no deeper than original root ball and tamp around stem firmly.

Soil: Banana grows in a wide variety of soils, so long as the soil is deep and has good internal and surface drainage. The ideal soil would be well-used compost. The effect of poorly drained soils can be partly overcome by layering stones or pebbles in the bottom of the planter. The plant does not tolerate poor drainage or flooding!

Insects: Spider mites, white fly and aphids enjoy sucking the nectar from banana plants. **Solutions:** Because of the leaf configuration, it is often dif-

Dwarf Banana (*Musa*)

ficult to spray effectively for insects. For complete eradication, you may need to rely upon a suitable systemic.

Diseases: The most common disease to affect banana plants is Fusarium wilt. **Solutions:** Destroy plant and discard soil, being careful not to infect other containers.

Health Benefits: Bananas contain large amounts of potassium and vitamin B6, in addition to providing ample amounts of magnesium, carbohydrates, vitamin C, riboflavin, biotin and fiber. Because bananas have a lower water content than most other fruits, they contain more calories and more sugar than other fruits.

The potassium in bananas is one of the most important electrolytes in the body because it helps to regulate heart function and fluid balance. These activities are prime factors in maintaining a healthy blood pressure. Various studies over the years have shown that potassium-rich foods are effective in lowering blood pressure and protecting against heart disease and stroke.

Bananas also contain a high amount of pectin, which is a water-soluble fiber that works to lower cholesterol, soothe the gastrointestinal tract and normalize bowel function. Studies have shown that plantain bananas may be effective in the treatment of peptic ulcers.

Ready for the Kitchen: Harvest bananas when they are fully colored and beginning to soften to the touch, usually about 75 days after formation or when the blooms at the end of the banana stalk begin to fade away.

Annual Savings: Approximately $47 per year per person on average.

Pruning:
The Kindest Cuts of All

Pruning is a strange word with even stranger connotations. It comes from the medieval French, *proignier*, meaning "to cut off superfluous twigs, branches and shoots." To modern gardeners, it means trouble.

Perhaps as few as five out of every hundred gardeners understand the necessity of pruning trees and shrubs (and, yes, occasionally smaller annuals) to keep them healthy and under control. Fewer still know the basic rules and tools for successful pruning and the terminology of the art.

At the mere mention of the word, many gardeners go into panic, conjuring up images of Mr. Brown — a middle-aged man balding at the crown and dressed in baggy pants, baseball jacket and tennis shoes — running electric shears over a row of outdoor hedges. In twenty minutes flat, he has carved away two-thirds of the shrubs' growth, dumped the twigs in the trash, hung the shears in the garage for use again next fall and plopped himself in front of the television to await the coming of winter. That's not pruning. It's lunacy.

Others envision Mr. Johnson, who lives down the block. He spends the entire spring cutting his outdoor shrubs and trees into perfect geometrical shapes — domes, triangles, squares, hearts — so that, by summer, his lawn looks like a box of hastily emptied Lucky Charms.

Still others, like Mr. Smith, view pruning as a lot of hooey. After all, Mother Nature put the plants here on earth. Certainly she can take better care of them than humans in all of our high-flying gardening wisdom.

Well, Mr. Smith is wrong — on two counts. In the first place, whatever shrubs and trees Mother Nature deposited on Mr. Smith's property were in all likelihood thinned or removed by humans in our never-ending quest for expansion. Thick forests were reduced to thin groves, then to occasional specimens and finally to barren fields as bulldozers and shovels clawed their way into the countryside. In the end, municipal employees and private citizens reintroduced most of the trees and shrubs after home construction ground to a halt. Mother Nature had nothing to do with that vegetation. At best, she was an adopted parent. Nor does she get any credit for allowing her creations to grow unchecked; *that* is not the goal of the typical homeowner.

Secondly, plants left to their own devices certainly *can* do quite well for themselves. Lighting, wind, animals, insects and diseases naturally "prune" broken or spindly limbs or even entire shrubs and trees. In that way, the weak perish and the strong grow ever stronger.

Unfortunately, humans, by and large, do not live in communal harmony with the woods and the forests. Our desires within our own community don't often correspond with the will of Mother Nature. Mr. Smith doesn't want a back yard that looks like an untouched national forest. He wants a few shade trees — tall enough to walk under without bending. He wants grass, a flower garden, vegetables growing off to one side, a few fruit trees lined neatly against the garage, a bird bath, a patio and perhaps a small herb garden right outside the kitchen door.

Mother Nature can't work miracles.

Likewise, the pruning approaches of Mr. Brown and Mr. Johnson leave something to be desired. Their attacks are wasteful and aesthetically defeating. There's nothing that's useful or attractive about uniformly clipped plants that are indiscriminately shaped regardless of their sculptural form.

Fortunately, there is a better way. And one that you can put into practice on your own container plants. Once you learn the secrets to successful pruning, you'll find the knowledge invaluable, whether working indoors or out.

To the indoor gardener, pruning is as important and necessary a procedure as watering, feeding and repotting. Once certain principles and procedures are learned, pruning is certainly no more difficult than confronting a bag full of plant foods and fertilizers and trying to determine which is the best to buy. But first you must understand the very basic objectives of pruning.

Objectives

The wisest pruning practice is the one that modifies growth of a plant to meet your immediate objectives without destroying the natural growth pattern or appearance of the plant. With very little effort, you can turn a beautiful and leafy citrus tree or blueberry bush into a scraggily, misshapen twig. All it takes is a pair of pruning shears and just the right amount of ignorance.

Some indoor plants require less pruning than others in order to meet your immediate or long-range goals. Some, in fact, require *none*. (Don't get too excited; there aren't many of *those* around!) Other plants, depending on their natural growth habit, require almost constant effort. You'll want to avoid the plants in the latter group unless you have plenty of time and patience (and just a touch of masochism) to devote to them.

Maintaining Plant Health: The first and most important objective in pruning container plants is to eliminate all diseased, broken and dead material. Easy enough. The reason you want this stuff out of your life is that, if left alone long enough, diseases could spread — or enter through wounds in the bark — and ultimately destroy the plant. Pruning is an effective preventive measure.

Eliminating Undesirable Growth: Trees and shrubs force-grown within the strict confines of a pot often tend to put out unattractive, awkward or even unhealthy growth. Pruning out all crossing branches, for instance, prevents possible rubbing and injury while opening up the inside of the plant's structure to allow more light to penetrate. This is a very desirable benefit to the plant, especially indoors, where ample natural light is rarely available. Thinning out weak, scraggly or dead branches is also important and can likewise improve the health of the plant, the quality of future foliage and — in the case of fruit and vegetable plants — the quantity and quality of blooms.

Controlling Plant Growth: Perhaps the most obvious objective in pruning container plants is to prevent them from growing out through the roof, which can be messy when it rains. Pruning does prevent plants from putting out too much undesirable growth, but, in addition, such "surgery" actually stimulates additional growth where it belongs — which is wherever you want it. In this sense, pruning is a bit like cavorting with the gods: you feel an intense sense of power and majesty in being able to alter, speed up or slow down the growth of some shoots and branches. However, the rewards do not come without a price.

Since container plants are totally removed from their natural environment, they're dependent upon you for their very life. That's especially true with indoor plants, which may be native to Madagascar, Burma, Australia, Greece, China, our own Rocky Mountains or Midwest. These specimens are so far removed from their natural habitats (which may include plateaus, mountains, forests and deserts — all grouped together) that it's easy to imagine that their growth might at first be sluggish, weak or even nonexistent. Careful, knowledgeable pruning habits can help restore some of the natural growth and vigor such plants enjoy in their natural environment.

Pruning's Effects on Plants

To understand the effects of pruning a tree or shrub, you must first understand what takes place *inside* the plant.

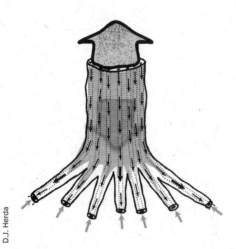

A typical tree or shrub is composed of four elements: (1) root system, (2) trunk and branch framework, (3) leaves and (4) propagating (seed-producing) flowers. All of these elements combine rather amazingly to produce growth. Yet each plays a unique role in the development of the plant.

Root System: These thin, fibrous, underground extensions serve to absorb moisture and raw materials (which are later pumped to the leaves and converted into food) and to act as a support and anchor for the plant, holding it firm against both wind and gravity.

Water and minerals in solution pass from the ground into the roots and throughout the trunk, branches and leaves via the tree's core. Manufactured food returns from the leaves to the roots via a layer under the bark.

D.J. Herda

Framework: All plants except the microscopic ones have a main stem structure. This consists, in most varieties, of a central trunk with auxiliary branches and sub-branches and is similar in appearance to a well-developed root system in reverse. As with roots, branches serve a double function. They hold the plant erect and in balance, and they act as a sort of plumbing system — much like your own home's plumbing system — that constantly moves matter up and down between roots and leaves. Water and minerals percolate upward through the core, or center, of the trunk and branches, and manufactured food seeps down through a membrane-like layer just beneath the bark.

Because, in our discussion of pruning, we'll be referring to certain terms, it would be a good idea for you to be aware of their meanings.

The "leader" is the name given to the one dominant branch that points skyward. Usually, it's the continuation of the trunk. "Scaffold branches" are the main side branches, usually the best-developed branches on the plant. "Lateral branches," which grow off the scaffold branches, are shorter and smaller. "Spurs" are the very short branches — actually stubs — that carry leaves, flowers or fruit.

Leaves: These fantastic "food factories" use energy from the sun to help carbon dioxide from the air combine with water percolated up from the roots to form sugars and starches that sustain the plant. Other substances from the roots and chlorophyll in the leaves also play a role in this reaction.

Each leaf consists of a broad blade, which is connected to a branch by means of a stalk, called a "petiole."

Under normal conditions, a plant has just enough roots to provide the leaves with raw materials for the manufacture of food. But when roots are reduced in volume — as occurs when a tree is transplanted into a container — the reduced number of roots are incapable of sending up the same amount of food-producing solution. As a result, the amount of foliage is reduced. (Less food means less growth.) Reduced foliage requires less work of the roots, which in turn send up even less solution.

Thus, whenever a plant's root system is reduced, the framework and leaves of the plant are similarly affected. The foliage should be proportionately reduced through pruning in order to maintain healthy, growing, well-balanced plants. This is one of the basic concepts of pruning

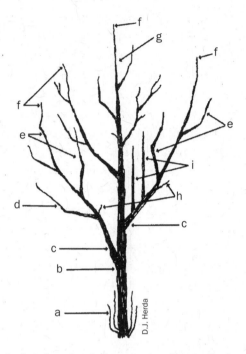

The pruning terminology for a tree's framework—its growth above ground: a) suckers, b) narrow or weak crotch, inclined to split as tree matures, c) primary scaffold branches, d) secondary scaffold branch, e) lateral branches, which grow from primary and secondary scaffold branches, f) terminal growth, which includes all growth from the end of a branch, g) leader, which is taller than all other branches, h) spurs, or short lateral branches that bear the fruit on most fruiting trees, i) water sprouts or "suckers."

and one of the most important things to remember. When a plant's roots are reduced in volume, the plant's foliage must be reduced proportionately.

Flowers: The flowers of most trees are attached to the branches. The only goal of the blossoms is to create seeds to be used for the species to perpetuate itself. Without the flowers, most plants would fade out of existence. Once properly pollinated, the blooms produce seed, which may vary in size from a microscopic speck to an avocado seed or a mango seed or the giant seed of the coconut.

Not all plants' flowers, remember, are conspicuous or especially decorative. Some are nearly impossible to discern from a distance of even a few feet.

The Growth Cycle

Each of these four plant parts — root system, framework, leaves and flowers — functions efficiently, precisely on cue. At different times of the year, roots, stems, leaves and flowers go to work in different ways to accomplish different tasks.

Springtime is the start of most plants' growing season. Food that has been stored in the roots and branches suddenly begins to flow. Roots begin a new season of growth, buds swell and burst open, and branches, leaves and flowers come to life.

If the plant is deciduous — that is, if it sheds its leaves in fall — it puts out all new foliar growth in the spring. If it is evergreen — that is, a cone-bearing evergreen or a flower-bearing evergreen such as the *Rhododendron* or one of the many tropical evergreens — it adds new growth to already existing foliage.

At first, spring growth is slow. The first few leaves come from buds formed the previous year. These new leaves immediately begin producing food to supplement the stored food, which is being steadily depleted. Finally, the plant sprouts enough leaves to sustain itself, and the source of food for growth shifts — almost as if an electrical breaker were thrown — from stored to manufactured.

The plant continues its growth throughout summer and generally into fall. As the cold weather approaches, even indoor plants sense the shifting of the seasons and gradually stop putting out growth. The roots remain active, though, absorbing life-sustaining nutrients and water to see the plant through the nearing winter and to store nutrients for the coming spring.

By late fall or early winter, the plant enters its dormant stage. At this point, water, food and any supplemental light you normally give your plants should be reduced, and the plants should be kept at a cooler temperature if possible. A plant will remain lethargic, much like a hibernating bear, until the arrival of spring signals once again the beginning of the plant's growth cycle.

Bud Growth

A bud is the point of the stalk where, given sufficient stimulation and proper circumstances, a new branch will begin to develop. It's important to be able to recognize a bud, because buds tell a gardener many things about the plant, including what you can expect if you prune the plant in a given location.

The terminology for buds is relatively simple. "Terminal buds" grow from the ends, or terminals, of branches. "Lateral buds" grow from beneath the terminal buds.

"Dormant buds" are simply buds that are not yet ready to respond to growth stimuli. They are generally smaller and less developed than terminal and lateral buds.

Where to Cut

There's only one proper place to cut back, or "head," the branches of shrubs or trees. That is immediately above a good, healthy, well-developed bud. What can you expect to happen when you make a cut in a branch? Let's look at an indoor maple tree to see.

In general, cutting back a branch affects only the growth of those buds in the immediate vicinity of the cut. If you make two cuts on the tree in Figure 3, three things happen.

- From the top bud (the new terminal bud) on each stub, a new stem develops. But the buds on each stem below the point of pruning remain inactive.
- Each of the new branches grows enough to maintain the balance of the tree. The branch on the left, from which you cut six inches, grows six inches, plus perhaps another foot to keep up with the growth of the tree as a whole. The branch on the right, from which you cut three feet, grows three feet, plus another foot to keep up with the growth of the tree. Therefore, the cut on the left branch stimulates a foot-and-a-half of new growth, while the cut on the right branch stimulates four feet of new growth.
- The four feet of new growth on the right branch produces many strong buds and new leaves. The foot and a half of new growth on the left produces smaller buds and fewer leaves. That's because more of the plant's food and growth hormones are directed to the side of the tree that has suffered the most damage (i.e., received the heaviest pruning), at the expense of the left side of the tree, which receives only minimal amounts of food and growth hormones. Other factors, too, come into play. But the important thing to remember is that, *the more severe the pruning, the more the plant responds to that pruning with new growth.*

Besides stimulating a plant's new growth through pruning, a smart grower can also determine the *direction* of the new growth. Look closely at the buds on a plant. Large or small, each points in a particular direction.

Either that direction is toward the center of the tree (an inside bud) or away from the center of the tree (an outside bud). *The way that bud is pointing* is *the direction in which the new branch will grow.*

Knowing this, you can determine in advance of pruning not only the direction in which a new branch will grow, but also the direction of growth you wish to stimulate. By pruning down to an inside bud, for example, you can make a new branch grow in toward the center of the tree to fill in any weak spots or gaps in the tree's structure. A nice cosmetic touch — and you did it yourself.

The effects of pruning can be seen in this illustration. The left-hand branch, pruned to point (a), will produce growth equivalent to that pruned away, plus a modest amount more. The right-hand branch, pruned to point (b), will produce growth equivalent to that pruned away—a much greater amount than with the left-hand branch—plus a modest amount more. It's apparent that heavier pruning stimulates more new growth than light pruning.

Such pruning also reduces new outward growth by forcing that growth inward, instead.

By pruning to an outside bud, on the other hand, you can make a branch grow outward. In this way, you can increase the general size of the plant and avoid crowding the inside framework.

Heading Back Versus Thinning Out

There are two basic pruning techniques. One is called "heading back," and the other is "thinning out." Heading back consists of cutting back branches to a bud, a technique used most often to control the size and growth rate of a plant. Thinning out is the *complete removal* of branches by cutting them away at the main trunk or a lateral branch.

Heading back usually results in a fuller, bushier plant, because the cuts, as we saw above, stimulate aggressive new growth from the new terminal buds. Thinning out produces the opposite effect. Such pruning opens up spaces within the framework of the plant and makes the plant more airy. Whether you thin out or head back depends strictly on the results you want to achieve in your pruning.

Summer Versus Winter Pruning

Light heading back — minor pruning — can be done at any time of year without harm to a plant, but heavier pruning should come at definite points in a plant's growth cycle.

Deciduous trees (those that shed their leaves in cold weather) should generally be pruned in winter, when they are dormant. At that time, leaf-holding stems and branches are inactive because the foliage has dropped, and the trees are feeding lightly from stores of food in the roots. That's the best time to prune back whatever wood you find undesirable.

Conversely, deciduous plants should not be *severely* pruned during the summer months, because that's the time when the plants are working to produce food not only for growth, but also for storage for the coming winter. They need those leaves during summer! If you greatly reduce the foliage at that time, the plants will be unable to produce and store enough food to see them through the winter months and the spring growth push. As a result, they could die over winter (winter "kill off").

Light summer pruning is valuable for some trees, such as figs, that bleed profusely if pruned in late winter or spring, when the sap begins to flow. However, the best time to prune such trees is in the fall or early winter, after food has been stored and before the sap flows again in spring.

Also, summer pruning is best for perennial plants. Winter pruning would remove much of the bloom-supporting growth, and fewer blossoms would result. So wait until

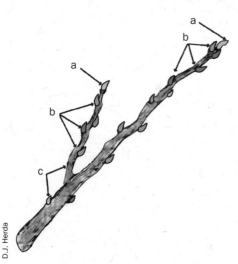

D.J. Herda

Bud terminology and bud growth direction: a) terminal buds; b) lateral buds; c) dormant, or undeveloped, buds. As one bud is pruned away, the new terminal bud will produce growth in the direction of the bud's tip.

after the blooming period is over (sometime in early summer), and then do whatever pruning is necessary.

Whether you follow a practice of light summer pruning or somewhat heavier winter pruning, remember not to clip too much from the plant at once. The prudent pruner follows the advice of architect Ludwig Mies van der Rohe: *Less is more.*

It's not how *much* you remove from a tree or shrub, but *what* you remove and *when* you remove it that counts.

01:00   IN A MINUTE

- Nearly all plants benefit from proper pruning, but fruit trees and shrubs profit more so than many others.

- You can help shape a plant's growth habit simply by knowing which branches to prune and where.

- Head back your plants to keep them short and thick; thin them out to open up the crown to sunlight and increased yields.

Dwarf Pomegranate (*Punica granatum*)

Habit: Tree

Cultivars: Several varieties are available, two of the best of which are:
- Nana and State Fair

Seed or Transplants: Transplants

Pot Size: Large to extra large

Water: This drought-tolerant plant requires only moderate watering. Allow the soil to dry out in between.

Comments: Pomegranates have been popular throughout human history and are currently undergoing a surge in popularity due to the health benefits associated with their juice. Widely grown for their edible fruit, they are equally valuable as ornamental plants. While their precise origin is unknown, pomegranates are considered native from the near-Middle East to the Himalayas. The first plants were probably introduced into the southeastern United States by early Spanish settlers to their colony at St. Augustine, FL. Pomegranates are often found around old home sites

Dwarf Pomegranate (*Punica granatum*)

and plantations, especially in the Midlands and Coastal Plain of the South. They grow and flower best in the arid regions of the Southwest, to which they are particularly well adapted.

Seeds: N/A

Transplants: Place in hole no deeper than original root ball and tamp around stem firmly.

Soil: Pomegranate plants are easy to grow and require little maintenance once established. They are adaptable to most soils, but they prefer a soil pH of 5.5 to 7.0 and require good drainage. Like most shrubs, they benefit from a 2- to 3-inch layer of organic mulch.

Diseases: Pomegranates are relatively insect- and disease-free and require little care in these areas.

Health Benefits: Pomegranates are higher in calories than many other fruits. But don't let that dissuade you from growing and eating them. They contain powerful anti-inflammatory antioxidants. Because they contain a high level of antioxidants, they are effective in helping to fight disease. They are becoming increasingly popular due to their high potassium content (often higher than in oranges). Studies have found that pomegranates slow the growth of prostate tumors.

Ready for the Kitchen: Harvest pomegranate when the fruits are fully colored, slightly swollen and medium soft to the touch, usually between late September and mid-November.

Annual Savings: Approximately $82 per year per person on average.

Tools of the Trade

Every gardener has tools to meet his or her own specific gardening requirements. But, while a complete selection of tools varies from person to person, there are some basic tools no container gardener should be without.

Pruning Tools

Several firms specialize in the manufacture of pruning tools. Other firms produce pruning tools as a sideline of general hardware. Both kinds of firms seek to protect their tools from duplication through adoption of various patents. To the buyer, this means that each tool — no matter how similar it looks to a competitor's tool — is slightly different, if only in construction or materials not readily discernible to the layman's eye. Only use can tell you which pruning shears, pruning saw or lopping shears you'll find most convenient and effective.

As pruning tools differ in style, so too do they differ in price. One word of caution: Don't buy cheap. In pruning tools, cheap is far more expensive in the long run. Whereas good-quality tools will last a lifetime with just a reasonable amount of care, most bargain-priced tools will last only as long as you don't need them. When the time comes for use, the spring mechanism invariably pops or the handle cracks or the blades don't mesh just right. As a result, bargain-priced tools cost time, money and very possibly your plant's life — not to mention the frustration that goes with trying to use inferior products.

Container gardening, luckily, requires fewer complicated pruning tools than does its in-ground counterpart. Only four items will generally see you through your container-garden pruning activities.

Pruning Shears

These come in two varieties, anvil and drop-forged. The anvil type has a single, straight-edged blade opposite a flat bed (or anvil) of soft metal. The advantage of the anvil is that its frame is generally constructed of rolled steel or aluminum, so the tool is lighter than a drop-forged shears of similar size. In my opinion, the anvil is also hardier, a consideration if you're especially rough on tools.

The drop-forged type is the older and generally more favored of the two shears. It has a steel cutting edge along with a thicker hook and works with a scissors-like action. When in good condition, this type of shears makes a good, clean cut perhaps an eighth of an inch closer to the parent branch than is possible with anvil shears.

Lopping Shears

For pruning branches larger than hand shears can safely or effectively manage, lopping shears come in handy. Generally, these tackle cuts up to an inch-and-a-quarter in diameter with relative ease. Standard care of loppers includes occasional oiling of the bearing and sharpening of the blade on a whetstone.

Pruning Saw

For cuts on branches larger than an inch-and-a-quarter (a rarity in container-garden pruning — though, with larger trees, it does occur), a pruning saw is necessary. This tool consists of a simple tapered, curved, toothed blade attached to a knife-like handle. The tool is lightweight and easily maneuverable even in tight spots. It bites on the pull stroke and does a fast, clean job. There's also a folding pruning saw with a handle that flips over the blade to protect the teeth when not in use. It's a useful tool to carry in your pocket or keep neatly tucked away in a drawer until needed.

Pruning Knife

For the lightest pruning needs, a small, sharp pruning knife is best. It, like the saw, has a curved, tapered blade leading to a knifelike handle. But it is, unlike a saw, toothless. Such a knife is also handy for disbudding roses and other flowers for cut-flower table displays.

(a) A good pruning knife pays off in dividends. Here, a container gardener is cutting several sections from a sweet potato for planting. (b) She prepares the potting soil for its company. Notice that it has already developed a sprout, which will speed its growth. (c) She places the cutting in the soil... (d)...and she covers it to just below the base of the sprout before tamping it down firmly with her fingers. (e) She gives the planting a generous dose of water with a mild mulch tea solution to help prevent transplant shock. (f) One month later, the vines are well developed. Next step: transplanting into a deeper container to allow for tuber growth.

Wound Dressing

Small cuts require no special attention, but larger cuts should receive a coating of pruning wound dressing. This protects the wound and keeps out bacteria and other disease-causing organisms while the wound slowly closes itself. Wound dressing comes under many different labels, is nontoxic and should be applied according to directions on the can. It's available at most nurseries and garden supply centers.

Care of Pruning Tools

Tools that don't work are worthless. Tools that work poorly, pulling and bruising branches that should be cut clean, are even worse. To keep your pruning tools in top condition, wipe all metal surfaces with an oily rag after each use.

To prevent rusting, oil all moving parts and bearings at least yearly. When your tools appear to be getting dull, have a professional sharpener hone them back to their original cutting efficiency. Unless you know what you're doing, saving money by sharpening them yourself usually means unevenly honed, unsatisfactory cutting edges.

Most of my own pruning tools are manufactured by Seymour Smith & Son, Inc. They're Snap-Cut brand, and I use them for one reason: they work. Year after year after year. That's not to say other manufacturers' products aren't worth trying. I've heard many gardeners talk about the durability of Wiss pruning shears, especially. Others may be just as good, although I personally can't recommend them. If someone you know can, that's the best reason in the world to try them.

Additional Indoor Gardening Tools

If you plan to collect and oven-sterilize your own soil, you'll find a small, sharp spade a blessing. I prefer one with a collapsible handle. You can pick one up at a camping supply shop, a hardware store or (probably cheapest of all) an Army surplus store. When not in use, the blade folds compactly against the handle for quick, easy storage.

If much of the soil you collect is lumpy with clay or stones, you'd do well to get a medium-mesh screen to sift the dirt before sterilizing. That way, you can screen out all the undesirables before potting time. Make sure the mesh is wide enough so that small pebbles — which are good for drainage and soil porosity — and small chunks of twigs and other organic matter pass through while the other objectionables are blocked. A common bricklayer's trowel is useful in pulling the soil back and forth across the screen.

Another "must" is a sturdy, two-gallon bucket — preferably one made of metal, not plastic. If necessary, the metal bucket can be used in the oven as a sterilizing pan — something a plastic one couldn't quite pull off. Make sure the bucket has a handle to aid in lugging soil. A small-capacity (about two-quart) watering can comes in handy for watering small cuttings, seedlings and hard-to-reach ground cover planted as companion plants to your fruits and vegetables. The can should have a tapered spout for that little extra "reach." To supplement it, a two- or three-gallon sprinkling can is a must. I prefer plastic, because it's just that much lighter than metal and doesn't rust. Use this can to water your large containers and, in between watering, to "age" chlorinated city tap water.

Finally, no container gardener should be without a good sprayer or mister for adding humidity to plants. You can get anything from a $1.95 plastic quart bottle with an adjustable nozzle that lets you dial from stream to mist all the way up to a battery-operated, electric houseplant sprayer complete with overnight charger. Don't laugh. I have one. (Although, admittedly, when I first heard of it, I laughed.) It's turned into one of my favorite gardening gadgets. Several different manufacturers make them. Other similar models are not rechargeable but instead run on batteries (which may be rechargeable: remember the environment!). Depending upon the power source, these units can be good for up to ten hours of spraying or more.

At the flick of a switch, the device delivers anything from a steady stream to the finest mist I ever saw come out of a nozzle.

Of course, these sprayers can be a bit pricey — ranging from $25 to $100 or more. But, if you're serious about your indoor gardening (and outdoors, too, for that matter), I think you'll agree they're worth the cost. If you have a lot of plants that require frequent misting, I highly recommend one.

Keep a manual pump-type sprayer around as a backup for when (not if!) your power sprayer gives out. These range in price from a few dollars to $40 or more, depending upon the size and complexity of construction.

As with other gardening implements, several manufacturers make reliable products in the sprayer-mister line. Not all are worth the price, though. I had one model that worked for only four months before a gasket broke and it failed to hold compression. After that, it leaked like a sieve. So buy wisely, preferably on the personal recommendation of someone you trust.

01:00 IN A MINUTE

- As an indoor gardener, you'll need to rely upon certain specialty tools from time to time—things you should have in your toolbox.

- The most costly tools you can buy are often the ones that have the lowest price tags and construction quality.

- Using the right tools for the right situation often marks the difference between success and failure.

Strawberries (*Fragaria ananassa*)

Habit: Spreading (running)

Cultivars: Numerous varieties of strawberry are popular, including:
- Earliglow, Tristar and Tribute

Seed or Transplants: Transplants

Pot Size: Small to large

Water: Give strawberries adequate water to prevent shriveling of the leaves, but allow to dry out between waterings. The plants will require more water while setting flowers and fruit.

Comments: Strawberries can be grown nearly anywhere. They are the first fruit to ripen outdoors in the spring, and no other small fruit produces berries as soon after planting as strawberries. In proportion to the size of the plant, strawberries are very productive. If 25 plants are set in the garden, these original plants and the resulting runner plants would produce a total of 25 quarts.

Growth Cycle: Strawberry growth is greatly affected by temperature and length of the daylight period. In new plantings, runner production occurs during the long days and warm temperatures of summer. In the short, cool days of fall, runnering stops and flower buds form within the plant crown, which is basically a compressed stem. The strawberry crown gives rise to leaves, runners and roots. The flower clusters that develop inside the upper portion of the strawberry crown in the fall emerge in early spring. Berries begin to ripen four to five weeks after the first flowers open and continue to ripen for about three weeks. Toward the end of the harvest period when the days are long and warm, plants once again grow runners that produce new plants.

Strawberries (*Fragaria ananassa*)

The performance of strawberry varieties can be affected by climate and soil type. 'Earliglow' is an unusual strawberry because of its wide adaptation throughout the United States and Canada. 'Earliglow' is also resistant to red stele. No chemical controls are effective for the home gardener for the control of this root disease. Planting a variety resistant to red stele is the safest and most effective means of dealing with this problem.

June-bearing Type: The name June-bearer is somewhat confusing since these varieties bear most of their crop in May. June-bearers produce a single crop in the spring.

Ever-bearing Type: There are everbearing or day-neutral types that produce a crop in the spring and another in late summer, continuing until frost in the fall. All of the everbearing strawberries advertised in nursery catalogs originated in the northern states; therefore, they succeed best in those areas and are very poorly adapted to the mid-South but make great indoor plants.

Some home gardeners follow the practice of commercial growers who treat strawberries as annuals. Plants are installed in summer or early fall, usually with plastic mulch. They are not allowed to make offsets. After harvest the plants are removed and a new planting made. The benefits are healthier plants, fewer weeds and larger fruit.

Seeds: N/A

Transplants: Place in hole no deeper than original root ball and tamp around stem firmly.

Soil: Strawberries are easy to grow in a wide range of soils and require little maintenance once established. They are adaptable to most soils, but they prefer a rich, loamy, well-drained soil with a pH of 5.5 to 7.0. Like most fruits, they benefit from a 2- to 3-inch layer of organic mulch.

Insects: Root weevils, aphids, mites, and slugs and snails are among potential insect pests. **Solutions:** Spray with insecticidal soap, and pick off and dispose of larger insects.

Diseases: Strawberries are subject to many diseases, including fruit rots (gray mold, anthracnose), leaf diseases (leaf spot, leaf scorch, leaf blight), crown diseases, root diseases (red stele, black rot) and viruses. **Solutions:** To help reduce problems, plant only certified disease-free plants, water only early in the day to discourage the formation of fungal diseases over-night and give mature, bearing plants plenty of room and ventilation. (Use a fan where practical.)

Health Benefits: Strawberries provide an excellent source of vitamins C and K, fiber and flavonoids. They also offer a very good source of vitamin B1, iodine, manganese and pantothenic acid. Strawberries are also a good source of vitamin B6, folic acid and biotin.

The flavonoids contained in strawberries are responsible for most of their healthful benefits. As with other berries, strawberries' anthocyanidins are their most powerful flavonoids. Anthocyanidins are responsible for the vibrant red color of these berries. Studies have shown that because of strawberries' unique flavonoid content, they are effective in protect-ing against inflammation, heart disease and cancer. Strawberries are also effective in the fight against macular degeneration and rheumatoid arthritis.

Ready for the Kitchen: Because strawberries vary widely in their length of time to maturity, pick them when fully red, regardless of size. Strawberries can ripen overnight, so visit the patch daily once ripening begins. Although strawberries are true perennials, you should replace plants with new ones as they begin to decline in production, which occurs usually after three years.

Annual Savings: Approximately $65 per year per person on average.

The Sky Is Falling:
Battling Urban Pollution

The next time you're in Paris (and I'm guessing, if you're like me, that won't be for another week or two), stop by the southern face of the Musée du Quai Branly. There you'll see mankind's latest effort to defeat urban pollution — the noise and heat and airborne particulates common to every urban environment. It's a sprawling wall of living plants — more than 8,600 square feet of them, in fact. The wall, constructed by designer Patrick Blanc, features more than 170 different species.

Something of a gimmick, you say? Hardly. It is, rather, a statement. It's meant to show how greenery (the original "green" movement) can not only coexist with an urban environment but also contribute to its effectiveness.

Blanc's wall of plants is one of the largest in a growing number of "plant walls" or "vertical gardens" taking root across the world, as architects search for environmentally friendly ways to create beautiful buildings. Some visionaries even believe that soon we could be harvesting our food from the places where we live and work. And why not?

Ken Yeang is a prominent young architect who has a passion for what he calls "vegitecture." When he talks about plans for building new farms to feed the people of the future, he dreams of building up, not out. His concept for "vertical farms" where residents could grow and harvest their food from the walls of their own homes sounds a little crazy but makes a lot of sense.

French President Nicolas Sarkozy recently asked ten teams of leading architects to re-imagine Paris as a city fully integrated with nature. The results included Roland Castro's team that suggested a sprawling, 250-acre park circled by skyscrapers and another concept by designer Richard Rogers for a series of rooftop gardens and parks that hang suspended above the city's railways. Other plans included urban forests and a network of vegetable patches.[27]

The designers claim that plants provide not only a more aesthetically pleasing alternative to other traditional building materials used in construction, but also additional benefits, including noise reduction, natural cooling, air purifying and a psychological shot in the arm to everyone who uses the buildings.

"They're living walls, and they come in all sorts of colors, not just green," Richard Sabin of BioTecture told an interviewer from CNN.[28] Sabin has created numerous living walls, including the medal-winning design at the gardens of the Royal Horticultural Society's Chelsea Flower Show in London.

"They can be flowering, edible — we have just completed a wall that incorporates all kinds of salads leaves, such as pak choi and lettuce," said Sabin. "The future applications are endless; we're looking at the possibility of harvesting biofuel crops and even using plants [indoors] for grey water filtration."[29]

Bringing nature indoors may also have overall health benefits. "The plants absorb toxins and have a really positive impact on air pollution," said Sabin. "NASA takes plants into space to help clean the air — it's cheaper and more sensible than air conditioning. The same principle applies here."[30]

Architects and builders have known for years that conventional building materials may well take a toll on the environment, as well as the overall health of the buildings' occupants. Concrete walls allow noise and heat to reflect back onto people, who block out the racket by closing all their windows and cranking up the air conditioning. Living walls of plants, on the other hand, absorb noise and heat, cool and refresh the air and look more inviting, so people open their windows to take advantage of natural ventilation, fresh air and soothing visual images once again.

But even that clean outside air is only the tip of the ecological iceberg when it comes to vertical gardens.

"We can…do special air purification walls for inside buildings," said Sabin. "They can actually drop the temperature by degrees, so you don't need air conditioning."

Another advantage the designer sees in living walls is that they offer developers a "significant carrot" with which to woo development control authorities when trying to get approval for new constructions. "There are massive plusses with planning," said Sabin. "The walls improve biodiversity. We can plant them with local species and even include solitary bee's homes in the design, which is something we really like to do — and Government officers really like it."[31]

In these times of green living and Al Gore, local authorities are quick to latch onto new designs that take into account climate change and global warming while they create a refuge for various species in the urban environment.

The technology required to sustain vertical gardens — which are often nothing more than massive container gardens stacked atop one another — is complex. Although humans have been using plants on their roofs to stave off rain and plants on their walls to cool the inside of their houses for centuries, they have never before taken on such massive urban projects. Huge expanses of living greenery require more than a little

wind-blown soil and a few cracks in the masonry. Providing an irrigation system to keep the plants watered is, in itself, a staggering undertaking. And then there is the need to keep the building walls from absorbing and transmitting the moisture and repelling root damage.

Such walls are typically constructed of a complex matrix comprised of plastic and metal, arranged in such a way as to provide air circulation and temperature control. The plants themselves are housed in pockets of plastic and are fed and irrigated via a sprawling network of plastic pipes. The entire system must

This office building in France is a prime example of the emerging art/science of "vegitecture."

be light enough to hang on the side of the building and strong enough to resist damage from wind and storms.

But urban vegitecture is not without its critics, most of whom complain that so massive a number of plants requires a huge amount of water and more than its fair share of maintenance over conventionally constructed walls. Sabin, though, is determined to prove them wrong.

"They can use a lot of water, but we've been working on systems that cut demand dramatically," he said.

"A maintenance contract typically involves three visits a year," he said. "Two of these will be pretty cursory if we get the plant choice right, and only involve changing a few filters and the odd dead plant. Then once a year we will do a more thorough overhaul.

"These aren't just the materials of the future; this is about now; about really bringing nature into our cities and true sustainability. I think that's inspiring."

As inspirational as vertical walls may be, they're far from practical for most container gardeners — even those living beneath the umbrella of urban sprawl in big cities such as New York, Chicago and Los Angeles.

Container gardeners *can* take advantage of their plants' natural propensity to absorb airborne toxins while generating oxygen and cooling our homes.

Placing pots in strategic locations around the exterior of your house — particularly on the southern and western exposures — invites planting a whole host of vines, from cucumbers and melons to squash, beans and peas. Adding a sturdy trellis to each pot gives the vines something onto which to crawl, keeping those pesky plant tendrils from worming their way into the siding of the building while helping to shade the building's walls from the ravages of Old Sol.

On the upper stories of multi-level homes, window boxes placed in strategic locations allow vining plants to trail downward toward their trellis-bound cousins and can be accessed from inside the window for food, water and harvest.

Potted trees and shrubs can also be relied upon to both rid the air of pollutants and bathe the wall in cooling shade. And when the trees need to come in to escape the bitter blasts of winter, simply slide them onto a rolling trivet or a dolly and move even the largest of the pots to its new winter quarters.

01:00   IN A MINUTE

- Crossing architectural design with vegetative gardening results in what some green-thumb designers call *vegitecture*.

- New urban developments utilizing container gardens on a massive scale are sweeping the building-and-design industries.

- You can use urban-design concepts and proven techniques to provide a greener, more environmentally friendly home environment.

Dwarf Fig (*Ficus carica*)

Habit: Tree

Cultivars: Several varieties are available, including:
- Blackjack, Negronne and Peter's Honey Green

Seed or Transplants: Transplants

Pot Size: Large

Water: Water container thoroughly, allowing the soil to dry out well between waterings. Fig trees have a highly developed root system and can stand prolonged periods of drought.

Comments: Grow in tubs or large planters. Figs require four or more hours of direct sunlight (eight are better) from a southern exposure window. Keep evenly moist. Average indoor humidity levels. Day temperature 75–80°F; night temperature 66–70°F. Will not bloom if light is too low. Produces yellow-green skin with sweet, amber flesh; also known as 'Italian Honey Fig.' It tends to bear two crops a year, with the fall crop being more reliable than the summer. The delicious, green-skinned fruit with honey-colored flesh ripens in mid September.

Seeds: N/A

Transplants: Place in hole no deeper than original root ball and tamp around stem firmly.

Soil: Although fig trees will grow well in a wide range of soil types, a deep slightly alkaline soil is preferred. Fig trees should not receive much, if any,

Dwarf Fig (*Ficus carica*)

plant food, which could encourage foliar growth at the expense of setting fruit.

Insects: Insects and diseases are rarely a serious problem on figs. Various wood-boring insects may attack weak or dying trees. Use good growing practices to keep the trees vigorous.

Health Benefits: Figs, which predate the Old Testament and are a familiar reference throughout the Bible (where would Eve have been without them?), contain large amounts of fiber, natural sugars and minerals and are an excellent source of calcium, potassium, magnesium, copper, iron and manganese. Due to their high fiber content, they are often recommended to nourish and tone the intestines. Because they are a good source of potassium, they are also effective in helping to control blood pressure.

Figs are among the most highly alkaline foods, so they are beneficial in supporting the proper pH of the body, which contributes to overall health.

But fig trees are more than the mere sum of their fruits: studies have shown that fig leaves have antidiabetic properties, too, and can actually reduce the amount of insulin needed by persons with diabetes who require insulin injections. Researchers have also found that fig leaves are effective in lowering levels of triglycerides. Results of test-tube studies revealed that the leaves of this relative to the mulberry tree inhibit the growth of certain types of cancer cells.

Ready for the Kitchen: Different varieties of figs vary greatly in time to maturity. Harvest figs for fresh consumption when their necks wilt and the fruit droops. If you notice a milky, latex-like material after picking, the figs are not quite ripe. For preserving, harvest the figs a few days before maturity. The milky secretion can be irritating to some persons, so you may consider wearing rubber gloves as you harvest the figs. Picking the figs before they become overripe will lessen insect and disease problems. Birds may feed heavily on figs (in fact, you can count on it). Picking early in the morning will decrease bird damage. Netting is available to protect fig bushes from feeding by birds, but it is seldom practical because of the difficulty in applying it to the atypical fig tree configuration. Figs may also be allowed to dry on the tree for eating all year long.

Annual Savings: Approximately $60 per year per person on average.

Resources

Web Sites

GardenGuides.com (gardenguides.com/) — Providing thousands of pages of detailed and extensive online information on plants, pests, gardening tips and techniques, gardening recipes, seeds and bulbs, gardening books, nurseries and landscapers, and more

GardenScape.com (gardenscape.com/GSResources.html) — Providing information resources for the home gardener and professionals in the gardening, landscape and nursery industries

iVillage Garden Web (gardenbazaar.com/directory/1-cat_list.html) — An exhaustive listing of online retailers organized by categories and areas of gardening interest

KidsGardening.org (kidsgardening.org/) — Offering informative and inspirational articles encouraging youngsters and families to garden together

National Gardening Association (garden.org/home) — Offering one of the Web's largest and most respected array of gardening content for consumers and educators, ranging from general information and publications to lessons and grants

OrganicGardeningResources.com (organicgardeningresources.com/) — Providing a wealth of non-commercial informative how-to articles on organic gardening and related subject matter

USDA National Agricultural Library (http://riley.nal.usda.gov)

Books

Cramer, James, and Dean Johnson. *Window Boxes: Indoors and Out.* Storey Publishing, 2004.

Herda, D. J. *Zen and the Art of Pond Building.* Sterling Publishing Co., Inc., 2008.

Joyce, David. *The Complete Container Garden.* Reader's Digest, 1996.

McGee, Rose Marie Nichols, and Maggie Stuckey. *McGee and Stuckey's Bountiful Container.* Workman Publishing Company, 2002.

Schultz, Warren. *Pots and Containers.* Barnes & Noble, 1997.

Spier, Carol. *Window Boxes.* Barnes & Noble, 1997.

Notes

1. Tina Vindum. "Master Your Great Outdoors: How To Make Yard Work A Super Fitness Work Out, by Tina Vindum." Husqvarna. masteryourgreatoutdoors.com/outdoor_authority/tina.aspx (accessed Sept. 7, 2008).
2. Judith Dancoff. "Gardening for Health." MedicineNet.com. Oct. 30, 2000. medicinenet.com/script/main/art.asp?articlekey=51498 (accessed Sept. 7, 2008).
3. Ibid.
4. Roger S. Ulrich. "Health Benefits of Gardens in Hospitals." Center for Health Systems and Design. 2002. greenplantsforgreenbuildings.org/attachments/contentmanagers/25/healthsettingsulrich.pdf (accessed Sept. 7, 2008).
5. Ibid.
6. Ulrich ·
7. Judith Dancoff. "Gardening for Health." MedicineNet.com. Oct. 30, 2000. medicinenet.com/script/main/art.asp?articlekey=51498 (accessed Sept. 7, 2008).
8. Ibid.
9. Ibid.
10. Ibid.
11. "Prostate Cancer and Diet." *The Progress Report*. Prostate Cancer Genetic Research Study. Spring 2005. fhcrc.org/science/phs/progress_study/newsletter/news2005_spsum.pdf (accessed July 1, 2009).
12. "Green Beans." *The World's Healthiest Foods*. The Mateljan Institute. whfoods.org (accessed July 1, 2009).
13. "Health Benefits of Apples." *EveryNutrient.com*. Every Nutrient. everynutrient.com (accessed July 1, 2009).
14. Marjan Kluepfel and Bob Lippert. "Changing the pH of Your Soil." Clemson University Extension. June 1999. clemson.edu/extension/hgic/plants/other/soils/hgic1650.html (accessed July 11, 2009).
15. Ibid.
16. Ibid.
17. Ibid.
18. Marjan Kluepfel and Bob Lippert. "Fertilizers." Clemson University Exten-

sion. June 1999. clemson.edu/extension/hgic/plants/other/soils/hgic1654 .html (accessed July 11, 2009).

19. Ibid.
20. Ibid.
21. "Onions." *The World's Healthiest Foods.* The Mateljan Institute. whfoods.org (accessed July 1, 2009).
22. Akira Asai, Masaru Terasaki and Akihiko Nagao. "An Epoxide–Furanoid Rearrangement of Spinach Neoxanthin Occurs in the Gastrointestinal Tract of Mice and In Vitro: Formation and Cytostatic Activity of Neochrome Stereoisomers." *The Journal of Nutrition.* The American Society for Nutritional Sciences. Sept. 2004. jn.nutrition.org/ (July 21, 2009).
23. M.C. Morris et al. "Consumption of Fish and n-3 Fatty Acids and Risk of Incident Alzheimer Disease." *PubMed.* NCBI. July 2003. ncbi.nlm.nih.gov (accessed July 1, 2009).
24. "Spinach." *The World's Healthiest Foods.* The Mateljan Institute. whfoods.org (accessed July 21, 2009).
25. "Some Broccoli a Day Keeps the Doctor Away." *Eat for Life: Cancer.* Institute for Food Research. Nov. 20, 2008. ifr.ac.uk (accessed July 21, 2009).
26. "Apricots." *The World's Healthiest Foods.* The Mateljan Institute. whfoods .com/genpage.php?tname=foodspice&dbid=3 (accessed July 1, 2009).
27. "Green walls: the growing success of 'vegitecture'" *CNN.com/Technology.* June 29, 2009. CNN. cnn.com/2009/TECH/science/06/28/green.walls/ index.html (June 30, 2009).
28. Ibid.
29. Ibid.
30. Ibid.
31. Ibid.

Index

About the Author

D.J. HERDA is an award-winning freelance author, editor and photo-journalist who has written several thousand articles, and more than 80 books, including *Zen and the Art of Pond Building*. He is an avid organic gardener and test grower and has been writing extensively about growing fruits and vegetables for over 40 years.

If you have enjoyed *From Container to Kitchen,*
you might also enjoy other

BOOKS TO BUILD A NEW SOCIETY

Our books provide positive solutions for people who
want to make a difference. We specialize in:

Sustainable Living ✦ Ecological Design and Planning

Natural Building & Appropriate Technology ✦ New Forestry

Environment and Justice ✦ Conscientious Commerce

Progressive Leadership ✦ Resistance and Community

Nonviolence ✦ Educational and Parenting Resources

For a full list of NSP's titles, please call 1-800-567-6772 or check out our web site at:

www.newsociety.com

NEW SOCIETY PUBLISHERS